Eating Mangoes

A Residential Treatment Experience

Lisa Elefant

DREAM TREK

MADISON

Copyright © 2012 Lisa Elefant
All rights reserved.
ISBN: 978-0615718705 (Dream Trek)
ISBN-13: 0615718701

Dedication

I read a news article in college. It referred to a high school friend's sister. The sister was found dead in her apartment after several days of missing commitments. Finally, her dad went to her apartment. He convinced the landlord to open her door so that they could check on the young lady.

What they found was devastating. This young adult sister of my high school friend was lying dead in her apartment. She died as a result of a heart attack. A heart attack from the strain of her bulimia. She had starved herself to the point of weakening her heart muscle. She had purged to the point of throwing off her potassium and other electrolyte levels. She then went into cardiac arrest. Alone. In her apartment.

In the news article her dad said that he didn't understand why his daughter had to die; her life was worth so much more than twenty pounds.

This is for all of us who battle with eating disorders and the question: Am I worth more than twenty pounds? This is also for those who stand with us in the battle: our family, friends, therapists, and sponsors.

Contents

Dedication
Author's Note

1	A Hot Mess	1
2	Some Explaining to Do	7
3	Missing Person	18
4	Running Away	34
5	Vitals	37
6	Angels	42
7	Run	48
8	Realizations	58
9	Some Peace and Quiet	69
10	Gourmet Dinner	79
11	Support	89
12	Mistakes	96
13	Anger	112
14	An Insider's Perspective	118
15	Reality Check	123
16	Shalom	135

Author's Note

Calling upon my own memory and journals I have complied this book. The individuals and treatment facilities spanned several years and have been consolidated with the intent to make the story more readable. The names of most individuals and treatment facilities have been changed to protect anonymity.

This book is not intended to glamorize the treatment experience or disease behaviors. It is intended to give insight into the experience of treatment and recovery. It is intended to tell a story of God intervening in my life. It is a story of God revealing himself to me, and my journey to embrace that offer of friendship.

Some of the stories are specific and potentially hard to read. This is not a how-to or an encouragement to individuals wanting to go further into their disease.

Enough of us have already lost our lives, lost dreams, and lost years due to these dreadful diseases. Let us refuse to lose any more precious things to these horrible addictions. Let these stories shine a light on these ugly things so that we may see more clearly and come together in understanding and regain our lives. Let this book be permission to dream. Let us dream of recovery and dream bigger than recovery to our more meaningful lives.

I had a therapist in treatment named Moe. She used to give me assignments between sessions. One week the assignment was to make a list of one hundred dreams. Big and small. Achievable and (seemingly) unachievable. So I did. Number thirteen is: to write a book. This is that book.

Chapter One: A Hot Mess

This last time that I came to residential treatment I was a mess. A hot mess. I had been in and out of the hospital over the five months prior for refusing to eat and stopping my meds. My skin was a malnourished grey color. I had been kicked out of the sober living house that I was renting a bed at. I was living off of credit cards in spare rooms of friends in two different states. I slept in my car, in hotels, and I even slept secretly in the basement of a friend who was out of town. It was awful. I wasn't even above stealing things from the Donation Bins at the library or churches.

I was extremely depressed from inconsistently taking my psychotropic medication and engaging in my eating disorder behaviors for months on end. I hadn't yet relapsed on drugs but I had tried and it was only a matter of time. I felt worthless and ashamed. I lay on the bathroom floor having chest pains and in a state of severe dehydration. I wasn't sure if I was having a heart attack. I wasn't sure if my body would stay alive until I got back into residential treatment. I knew I was putting extreme amounts of stress on it daily.

I had been to residential treatment before and always found a new bottom I was willing to hit after I discharged. *God, this time I swear I will listen. I will do whatever I need to, just let me stay alive and make it back to treatment to get help. Please.*

Obviously, God graciously granted that request and I went back to residential treatment for (hopefully) the last time on July 3[ed].

I woke up my first day in treatment and I felt terrified to be awake. The weight of all the hours of "doing life" ahead of me was suffocating. I felt overwhelmed. Just putting my feet on the floor and walking to the bathroom felt like too much. That would be committing to be awake for the day and I wasn't ready to do that. Post

Traumatic Stress Disorder (PTSD) and Bipolar Type II was what they called it. Anorexia Binge/Purge Type, Chemical Dependency, and Self Injury were the maladaptive coping skills that I had become addicted to using.

Post Traumatic Stress occurs when there is an actual or perceived life-threatening situation and an individual remains stuck in the fight-or-flight response. Instead of passing through fight-or-flight and coming back to stop at a state of rest, an individual is trapped in the activated and extremely anxious state. This is what happened to me after my cousin died.

In the absence of my biological family, my friends who loved God had been standing beside me the whole time. They had been having the hard conversations with me, telling me to get help.

It was my senior year in high school. I entered in the back door of my house after seeing an evening movie with a friend. My mom met me on the stairway. She was crying. "Mark died," she said. After a moment of shock I said, "What?! What do you mean? That doesn't make any sense." Mark was my nineteen-year-old cousin.

As the hours passed by we found out more information. Mark was at a party. He had a bad trip on mushrooms. He had tried to crash his car into the ditch. After he survived the crash he had gone across the street to an open garage. In the garage he had suffered a bodily injury so severe that he had bled to death.

Mark's death horrified me. It haunted me. My dad had rationalized, "God blinked. That's the only way such a horrifying thing could have happened." This caused me to feel terror. *God can blink? Is that a real thing? Why do I deserve to be alive and not Mark?* I thought.

I felt like my own heart was bleeding and I was trying to catch the blood pooling in my hands but it was too much and it was spilling over. I wasn't equipped to handle the situation. I turned to self-injuring as a way to cope.

Others watched on and told me something was wrong. "Normal people don't cut themselves. Your body is a valuable creation of God," they said.

I felt like screaming at them, "Yes, I know something is wrong! I don't know how to fix it and I am too busy trying to catch the dripping blood. I would prefer if you could just leave me alone now. It doesn't help for you to stand there watching this mess. This is the only way I know how to cope. Don't tell me I am doing it wrong if you don't have a solution! I'm in a crisis here!"

In response my friends prayed. Not because I was nice or deserved it or asked for it, but because they loved me and they knew that prayer changed things.

My cuts and my scars spoke for me. They were a map of the pain that I had felt. They showed my anger and frustration at being gypped of a home and a family. They showed my fear regarding the future, my confusion about the present, and the brokenness of my past. They marked my self-hate, my desire to destroy and punish myself, my struggle to know if I wanted to live or die. They showed my feelings of chaos, my loss for words, and my desperation to be independent and to be okay. I was proud of my scars, ashamed of my scars, and afraid of my scars. I often wished they were deeper or worse, more extensive or more recent, more visible or more dramatic. I wanted them to match the amount of emotional turmoil I had felt. My scars were a reminder of where I had come from. My scars were wounds of a battle that I was fighting. I was struggling to cope with everything and to stay alive.

As my friends prayed to Jesus for my healing things

in my life began to unravel even more. I continued to make choices to do life all alone. I used the treatment center and my therapists as my Higher Power. Even though I believed in God factually, I didn't live like it practically. I was angry with God (whoever He was). I didn't trust that He was good anymore: How could God be good if my cousin died the way that he did? As is God's nature He was patient with me and continued to show me that He did love me over and over again.

I heard the still small whispered voice of God in answer to my question. I asked, *How could God be good if my cousin died the way that he did?* God said, *How could I be good if my Son died, bloody and nailed to a tree, the way that he did? How could I* not *be good?*

Chapter Two:
Some Explaining to Do

I walked into the phone room. There were eight phones for thirty-five women. Somehow it worked out surprisingly well most of the time. I sat down and used a Lysol wipe to disinfect the phone. I wasn't sure if that was a habit picked up from having lived with so many women in treatment or if it was part of my obsessive need for cleanliness.

Who should I call? What will I say? Thoughts passed through my mind like twigs floating downstream. I missed feeling like I belonged somewhere. I missed my friends that were my chosen-family. My biological-family had disintegrated when I was seven and my parents divorced.

I dialed the number to some friends from Wisconsin that I was close to. They didn't answer.

What would I say even if they did answer? I thought. *How would I explain what residential treatment was like? How would I explain what it was like to recover from an eating disorder and other addictions?*

My body was changing and I ignored the jeans that fit tighter around my waist; I left them in the back of my dresser drawer. I decided that I should probably get rid of them; they were my "sick pants," the ones that only fit comfortably when I was in the throws of my eating disorder. Yet, there was still part of me that wanted to hang onto them. *If only I could fit into them and be in recovery. Then,* I thought, *I'd be really happy with my life.* Thank god I had brought a bunch of leggings. This was precisely why leggings and yoga pants were so common at eating disorder recovery treatment centers.

I could have tried to tell my friends what it was like to be watched and evaluated every moment of the day. I could have tried to explain what it was like to ask to use the bathroom *every* time I needed it, because it was monitored so that we were less likely to vomit or self-injure in there. I could have tried to explain what it was like to have to ask to use the laundry room and to have to wait for phone times to call someone. I could have tried to explain what it was like to go through pocket checks and attendance rounds. It just seemed like an awful lot to try to explain. It wasn't so bad once I got used to it; I just tuned it out.

We got our food and had to check in with a Mental Health Counselor (MHC) by giving them our dietitian-approved menu. The MHCs made sure that we had the correct proteins (pros), starches (chos), and fats on our plate. Then we could sit down to eat.

I had seen girls toss food in the bottom of the toaster, in napkins and into the trash, under the table, into a cup of coffee and then not drink the coffee, under the edge of a plate, or outright edit their menu in line to indicate less food was required. The possibilities to restrict and get rid of food were endlessly creative. I was not judging, because I was not proud to admit that I did partake in attempting to restrict in some desperate ways in the depths of my disease. Eating disorders are a disease of desperation. That is part of the reason why they kill.

"Lisa? Are you Lisa E.?" said a woman with long dark

hair. She peered into my room.

I looked up and nodded, *Yes, I am Lisa E.*

"I am Anka, the Eating Disorder Specialist," she continued. It sounded more like "Eye 'am Ahn-Kah. Dee ee-ting dees-orter spea-chalist." She had a beautiful Belarusian accent. "Cah-n wee meet?" she continued.

"Yeah," I mumbled and slid off the bed. My brain was on overload since arriving at residential treatment; it settled somewhere around numb for the time being.

We walked to an empty group room and I took a seat. *She's foreign,* I thought, *she probably won't understand half of what I say. I don't have an eating disorder, definitely not since early college, so this should be a quick meeting.*

"Hi," Anka said as she gave me a warm smile and sat down. There was something so disarming and motherly about her. I decided that I liked her immediately. She reminded me of the friends I had made while volunteering in Romania several summers ago.

Anka explained that everyone who came into treatment got an eating disorder screening. "So what brings you to treatment?" she asked.

I half-smiled, gave a fake laugh and started right in, "I... um... well, I keep overdosing and a lot of the time I want to die… and I struggle with self-injuring."

"Okay," Anka said as she nodded and scribbled notes on the sheets of paper in front of her. For the next twenty-five minutes Anka proceeded to ask all about my food-life and history with food. Was I a picky eater? Did I binge or purge? How often? Did my parents have eating issues? Did I drink diet soda? What was my lowest weight? My highest weight? How old was I when I first noticed that I had eating issues? Did I have food preferences or foods that I didn't eat?

Normally, I would have been extremely guarded in my answers. Yes, I was a picky eater. No, I didn't binge. I used to purge; I was fine now. Yes, I drank diet soda – it was a staple of my diet. I didn't know my lowest or highest weight. I had stopped eating when my dad moved out of our family house when I was seven. Yes, I had foods that I refused to eat. Usually, actually, I ate only the same six foods in various forms.

For some reason, I let my guard down with Anka. I wasn't sure if it was her endearing accent or my belief that she wasn't going to pick up on a lot. Maybe it was just my biased assumption that she would struggle with my English and what a normal food-life in the States (as opposed to Belarus) looked like.

We got finished and Anka leaned forward in her chair. She clasped her hands and took a breath. "Lisa," she said (which sounded like "Leesah"), "I am sorry to tell you this, but you do have an eating disorder." Tears unexpectedly started to well up in my eyes.

"Wait. What?" I said. *Shit*, I thought, *I told her something wrong. What could I have said wrong? I minimized. I gave short answers. I made it sound like it was all in the past. I counted on her not catching my mistakes; I don't know what exactly constitutes an eating disorder anyway!* The only thing I could hear ringing in my hears was what a friend at home had said to me, "You don't have a real eating disorder. You make it look bad for people who *really* struggle with legitimate eating disorders."

I tried to explain to Anka, "No, you don't understand. I eat. I don't throw up anymore. I'm not underweight. Yeah, I am a runner and I am a bit obsessed with my times and miles and workouts, but that's *normal*."

"Leesah," she said, "eye 'am positeev about thees. You 'ave an eeting dees-orter. If I wah-sn't sure eye would say 'needs fur-thur eeval-you-ation.'" Tears started pouring down my cheeks. I didn't understand it. I wasn't even trying to get away with something. I was just trying to explain that I didn't have a legitimate eating disorder. I felt so ashamed that I had somehow misrepresented myself and now this foreign lady didn't understand that I really didn't have an eating disorder. Maybe I used to be headed down that road, but now I was in the clear.

I was irrationally angry with God for putting me in a treatment center that would trick me with a sweet foreign lady who told me that I have an eating disorder. *God, I prayed, do you even know what eating disorders are? Are you even here with me?* My anger and resentment spurted out in angry prayers like a fire hydrant being uncapped. As tear-lines slowly dried on my cheeks I felt a quiet spot in my heart develop. Quieter than a whisper I heard, *I'm here. I'm here and I do know what eating disorders are. They are not from Me. They are not from the One who Loves. Let me heal you.*

I was still angry. I responded with silence, but I felt better knowing that I wasn't alone.

"There's yogurt on my meal ticket. Can I switch it to milk?" I asked a MHC at lunch.

"No," the MHC responded, "We don't usually allow changes without the dietitian's approval."

"I can't eat yogurt," I said.

"Why not?" the MHC asked.

"It has bugs in it," I answered.

News got around to my treatment team about my belief that florae (or the good-for-you bacteria) in yogurt were "bugs." It was kind of funny, except that I truly refused to eat yogurt because in my head it was the same as eating bugs. My dietitian said, "I'm not sure if that's an anxiety/phobic thing or an obsessive compulsive thing or an eating disorder thing, but most people don't see yogurt as having bugs in it and refuse to eat it." I nodded. I didn't know either. I just knew that things like this controlled my life. And that part wasn't funny.

A woman with short brown hair walked up to me shortly after breakfast one day in the dining hall. "Hi, I am Adelina" she said. "I am the Addiction and Substance Abuse Specialist. I would like to do an assessment with you. Would you be available after the next group?" she asked. I nodded slowly, while my mind rapidly searched for the secret reason she wanted to meet with me. I thought that there had to be a secret reason because I couldn't think of an obvious reason. There was no reason she would need to meet with me; I wasn't an addict or an alcoholic.

We did the assessment shortly after the next group. "How often do you drink? Have you used marijuana? Cocaine? Opiates? Prescription drugs? Benzos? Have you ever been in legal trouble? Has anyone ever criticized you for your alcohol or drug use? Do you ever start out with a drink in the morning? Have you ever lost a job due to your alcohol or drug use?" The questions that Adelina asked went on and on and on. Finally, she finished.

"Lisa, you fit the criteria for Chemical Dependency," Adelina said to me. My heartbeat quickened and it felt hard to breathe. I put my hands on the side of the chair and pushed myself into a more upright position.

"No, you don't understand," I said. I didn't even tell her about my old roommates hiding all the medications in the house from me for the past year. I didn't tell her about driving while high on benzos and over the counter meds. I didn't tell her about being taken to detox two times after I overdosed (in my mind it was a mistake and totally unnecessary). I didn't tell her about calling my friend fourteen times during his grandpa's funeral and not remembering it. I didn't tell her about being listed as a missing person or switching benzos with Claritin to try to hide how much medication I was consuming.

"That can't be," I said. "I haven't done half the drugs on that list. I haven't been arrested. I'm not on Suboxone. I've never shot up."

"I know," Adelina said in a compassionate and understanding tone. "There are always not-yets that we think indicate that we don't yet have a problem. We have to look at what drugs and alcohol *have* done to damage our lives."

I felt close to panic by this point. My dad was a "recovering" alcoholic. His "recovery" wasn't something I respected much or aspired to emulate. I didn't want to be an addict. I didn't want to need the twelve steps. I didn't want to need recovery. I was afraid my life would be just like his; I wanted so much more. Hopelessness settled in the pit of my stomach. Despair rose to spread throughout my chest. *This is hopeless,* I thought. *What the fuck. I came to residential treatment because I have been self-injuring for nine years and chronically suicidal. I wanted there to be hope. Now they're telling me something is hopelessly wrong with me.*

I left the meeting with Adelina. Despair was fueling my actions. I asked to be let outside to take a walk around campus. Instead of walking around campus I walked straight towards the driveway exiting the treatment center campus. *Fuck this*, I thought. *I need something to calm me down. A razor to self-injure and a diet soda. Then maybe I can think.* As I walked memories flooded my consciousness.

Chapter Three: Missing Person

The night slid forward like the foot of a runner on fresh mud after a spring rain. Things were messy and slow. The terrain was unfamiliar and unkind. I rode the bus home that night. As we neared my dorm the bus stopped and I stepped off of it into the fresh air. Night had fallen and autumn was here. The air felt crisp to my lungs and the cool breeze on my face was refreshing. I stepped slowly in the direction of my dorm, concentrating every ounce of energy I had into staying calm.

Thoughts flew lethargically through my head. *I can't do this. I am a failure. No one would notice if I wasn't here. None of this matters. The only thing I do is hurt people.*

I tried to slow this stream of painful thoughts flying through my head but they rushed on like a freight train that has lost its conductor. My hands lay clenched near my waist around the straps of my backpack; I unclasped one and pulled open the door to the dorm lobby. As I fumbled for the keys to unlock the second entrance door I verbally encouraged myself, "Lisa, you can do this."

I listened to my sneakers squeak against the linoleum tiles on my way toward the stairwell. I stared at the corner where the floor meets the wall as I walked down the hall, avoiding the eyes of all whom I passed. I took the two flights of stairs a pair at a time to the second floor.

My mind circled through a plan for what I was going to do next. My roommate wouldn't be home. She would be out studying. I had a bottle of extra strength Tylenol, a bottle of ibuprofen, and a box of sleeping pills. I had one bottle of vodka that was almost full.

I walked past two girls sitting in the hallway having a conversation about the party they went to last night. They laughed loudly and it grated on my nerves. My face gave a half smile as I stepped past their conversation place. It took every ounce of energy in my chest to fake a smile.

The door to my room was plastered with clip-art pictures from our floor leader and random photos of my roommate posing with her friends. I didn't understand how she had friends, she wasn't nice to people and she wasn't happy. We lived together but communicated very little.

I unlocked the door to my room and quickly shut it behind me. Silence enveloped the small space and I quietly put the bottle of vodka and the pills into my backpack. I did this methodically and with slow intentionality. I couldn't sit down and rest for fear that I would lose my courage. My computer remained off and my room practically untouched as I turned to leave my room for the last time. Scenarios of the upcoming events played out rapidly in my mind.

If I overdosed in my dorm room there was the chance that my roommate would come home or I would chicken out and leave to get help. If I sat in the back stairwell there was the chance that someone would walk down the stairs and see me. Either way, someone I knew might be the one who found me after it was all over. I couldn't bear the thought of being responsible for the pain and distress of one more person. I had no other options; I needed to leave my dormitory to kill myself.

The last several weeks – years for that matter – had climaxed to this night. I just couldn't do life anymore. Everything caused pain to echo through my body. My chest hurt every time I took a breath; the stress was causing my body to tighten. Snippets of conversations from the past week replayed in my head. Angry faces, fighting words, and painful memories paraded through my mind like images on a slideshow, each one giving fuel to the rage inside of me. This rage strengthened my courage and solidified my resolve to follow through with this night.

I put on another layer of clothes over my sweatshirt and trudged down the hallway to the back stairwell. My steps echoed off the concrete in an offbeat sound of movement. As I descended down the stairs I felt my heart begin to beat quickly and adrenaline continue to pump through my limbs. I pushed open the heavy metal door leading to the back of the dorm building. Once again I felt the cool air rush past my face and heard the crunch of the fall leaves underneath my shoes.

I sat on the first picnic table I came to on the concrete patio behind the building. It felt good to sit down, but the rest didn't settle my nerves or lessen my feelings of distress. I unzipped the largest pocket of my backpack and took out the bottle of vodka. Quickly I took several long gulps of the vile-tasting liquid that brought numbness. This would give me courage and lessen the chances that I would falter in my plans. I quickly took several more long gulps of alcohol. Thirty seconds later I felt the vodka kicking in.

My mind began to move a bit slower and a wave of emptiness began to splash over the panic, fear, and pain that surged though my body. Everything was going to be okay soon. The pain was going to end. The pain was finally going to end. The plan was to drink until I knew I would black out and swallow all of the pills in my backpack just before I could no longer function. That way there would be no backing out.

Knowing the pain was going to end allowed me to exhale a little of the tension that I had been holding until now. I heard myself sob and gasp for air a couple times; it was painful to know I was about to end my life. This was the best thing to do right now. I caused everyone I cared about pain and I hated my life; I would be helping everyone if I just removed myself from this life.

Tears streamed down my face as I processed what was about to happen. What if I failed at trying to die, too? Would there be someone to love me? Was it a forgivable action to try to kill myself? What if I tried to die and ended up in a hospital alive and alone? A bolt of fear shot through my stomach. That would be continuing this living nightmare that was already in motion.

I took my cell phone out of my pocket and scrolled through the list of names in my directory, taking swigs of vodka intermittently. I called my best friend.

On the third ring she answered, "Hello?" I stalled and tried to think of the question I needed to ask her. I heard her ask again, "Lisa, can you hear me?"

I closed my eyes and started to speak, "Hey." I opened my eyes and began to walk slowly around the dorm building, holding the bottle of vodka in one hand and my phone to my ear in the other. "I need to ask you a question."

My best friend sounded confused, "Okay… Hey, Lisa, you sound a little funny. Are you doing okay?"

I fought to find clear words to say what I wanted to, "I just need to ask you a question. If something happened to me, would you come visit me in the hospital?"

There was a long three-second space of silence that lay heavy between us. "Lisa, what are you talking about? What is going on?"

I could hear panic entering her voice. *Shit, she can probably hear that I am already slurring my words. Fuck.* "I just need to know if you would come to the hospital and be with me if something happened," I said.

"Lisa, are you saying something is going to happen? Are you going to do something to yourself? I am going to get you help, okay?" I heard her start to cry as she finished talking. *That is odd,* I thought, *she never usually cries when I talk to her, even if I tell her I feel like I want to die. Maybe she can hear how serious I am this time.*

I could hear her typing. "Lisa, I am going to get help. I am instant messaging someone to call Peter. He is a pastor and he will know what to do." Peter was our youth pastor at church. He was aware of my depression and feelings of hopelessness, but they didn't train pastors in how to fix someone's life when it has been shattered into a thousand pieces.

"No, no, that's not what I need right now," I said. "I just need to know if you will be there. I need you to be there. Don't call anyone, please. Please don't get anyone else involved." The only consoling thing about my best friend having called Peter was that it meant she was not thinking of calling my parents. She and Peter knew that involving my parents would not be of any help; they were part of the problem.

"Lisa, I have four people calling Peter. I think he is playing basketball after church. He doesn't have his phone on him. Lisa, where are you? Are you at your dorm?" my friend asked.

"No, I'm outside. I will leave if you call anyone. I can't do this. I am really sorry," I said. I knew I was being difficult and I felt like I didn't have a choice. I sat on a wooden picnic table near the other end of the dormitory building. I was near the big trash bins. It was a little more secluded there. I opened my backpack and got out the bottle of Tylenol. I began counting out pills and held them in my hand. "I will leave if you send someone to come find me," I told her. I was already overwhelmed and someone else getting involved at this point did not seem like a calming scenario. It seemed like it would only cause more stress.

I began to get annoyed with my friend. She was trying to alter my plans to end the pain. There was no one that I would allow to enter into this situation if I could do anything to stop it. I felt too vulnerable. I felt so much pain already. I was too ashamed. I began to walk towards the back of the dorm building again. "I need to go," I said and I hung up the phone. I sat down on the street curb.

All of the sudden I heard someone say my name. "Lisa. Lisa, it's me." I looked up and stared at a lady who was slowly approaching me. "Lisa, it's me. Are you okay?" She said. *Why did she keep saying my name like I should know her? I had no idea who this lady was.* My mind was thick like molasses. The world was blurry and I felt nauseous. "Lisa, it's me." I squinted and stared hard through the darkness to try to see the face before me. *Oooh, I do know you*, I thought. *You are friends with my best friend. Fuck. She must have told you.*

I got up and started to walk away. The anger I felt trickled through the curtain of numbness that I had tried to construct. The lady followed me across the street and down the block. I walked faster and thought: *I need to find a place to take the pills before I am stopped. I can't do this. Everything is getting worse and more stressful. I just need this to end.*

I walked nearly a mile while being followed by this lady and all the while she was pleading with me to stop. She tried desperately to talk sense into my mind. I was way past my emotional and mental limit of coping. Everything inside of me had shut down. I felt that I had nothing left. We stopped for a minute to breathe and rest. My mind was reeling with the alcohol and my stomach was threatening to throw up its contents.

I was walking towards downtown, hoping I would lose my rescuer. I turned a corner and walked into the entranceway of a church courtyard. I sat down behind the brick wall and hoped that the lady would past me. I pulled my backpack around to my front and took out the pills again. My rescuer suddenly appeared and flung herself on me. I fought back. Those pills were my ticket to freedom from pain and hell. There was nothing I needed more in the world right now. She could not have them. We fought on the ground for a while until she took hold of all of my belongings. *Fuck. Fuck.* I thought.

It had been over two hours since I first called my best friend. The alcohol was starting to wear off a bit. Things were a little less blurry. I saw a car drive by us slowly. I realized it was my mom. Rage once again enveloped me. I got up and walked down the block away from her car; it was a one-way street and she couldn't follow me. *Someone has called my mother??* I thought. I couldn't believe someone would have called her. *This is ridiculous. My parents suddenly want to show up and be there for me? Well, it is too late. I am so angry. And I don't even have my pills or my vodka anymore,* I thought.

"Lisa, your mom has called the police. You are listed as a missing person. You can't keep running like this." I hadn't realized that my follower had been on the phone with various people most of the time that we had been walking. I felt like I was just waking up and coming out of a daze. The alcohol must've been wearing off a little.

I couldn't do this. Where was I going to go? I saw a police car drive slowly by. Suddenly I saw the break lights come on and the car did a U-turn. I had nothing left. My follower convinced me to sit with her on a bench that we happen to be passing. We sat for the next thirty-seconds and waited while the police officers got out of their car and walked towards us. "Lisa? Is your name Lisa?" they asked.

"Yes, this is Lisa." I heard the lady with me answer.

I was so ashamed. I couldn't look up from the ground. *Thank god I am still drunk,* I thought, *this is a fucking nightmare.* One police officer stood next to me as the other took my follower across the street to talk. After a couple minutes I saw her hand my backpack and things over to the officer. He began to walk back towards us. The other officer had been trying to talk to me. I did not comprehend the gravity of the events happening, but I was still able to sense the awkward tension that was between this man and I. He didn't know whether to try to joke with me, interrogate me, or lecture me. Finally he opted to just stand with me in silence. I appreciated this thoughtfulness.

The first officer walked back over to us and asked if I would like to go to my mom's house. My other option was to go to the hospital. "I'd rather go to the hospital," I said. I couldn't imagine spending the night with my mother – I was half drunk and the secret of my pain was spilling out tonight for her to see. By its very nature this night revealed the deep pain and turmoil that I felt. The police officer told me that my response was anticipated and my pastor had agreed to have me driven there for the night.

I was in shock. He cared enough about me to have me dropped off at his house in the middle of the night? I walked with the police officers to their car and got in. The digital clock on the dashboard read 2:20am. We drove in silence to Peter's house.

Shortly before arriving one of the officers breached the silent divide. "You know, you are really cared about." I stared out the dirty window at the houses we passed by. "You have a lot going for you," the officer continued to calmly talk to me. "I really wouldn't want you to end your life." I felt a little stab of shame when he said that sentence. It was still weird for me to have other people know that I felt like I wanted to die. "There are a lot of people who don't want you to do that."

I disregarded this sentence. *How did he know what people in my life wanted? He must not be aware that I only leave pain in my wake,* I thought.

"You are a really nice person."

He had only seen me drunk and in a state of having given up; he has no perspective of how nice I am, my mind continued its autopilot commentary. Nevertheless, I took what he said as a small complement.

"You know, I have a little baby at home, and there is something special about life." We pulled into the driveway of my pastor's home. "I want you to take care of yourself alright?"

"Okay," I heard myself say.

I was nearly shaking as I waited for the officer to step out of the car and open my door. The front light to the house was on. We walked together up the steps. The officer was holding my backpack. My pastor met us at the door and stepped onto the porch.

"Hi. My wife is sleeping; I'm just going to step out here to talk."

"Are you Peter?" he asked. Peter nodded. "Thanks for doing this," he said.

"Oh yeah, well, we care a lot about Lisa. It seems like this is an unusually rough night," Peter replied.

The officer wrote down his address and phone number. He then told us good night and handed the backpack to my pastor, asking him to keep it in his possession until the morning.

As the officer left we stepped into the living room. I was so ashamed; I could not look up from staring at the ground in front of me. I stood in the entryway staring at the floorboards.

"Lisa, come here. Sit on this chair," he said. I followed his instructions, not looking up from the ground. Peter squatted down in front of me, "Lisa, I need you to agree to three things if you stay here tonight. Can you do that?"

I couldn't speak. I merely nodded. I was still memorizing every detail of the hardwood floors.

"I need you to agree to not take anymore pills, to not drink anymore tonight, and that we will go talk to a counselor together tomorrow morning. Can you agree to those things for tonight?"

I nodded.

"Lisa, look at me," he said. I couldn't. "Lisa, just look at me." I couldn't. "Just look at me for a second," he said. My eyes stared at the floor out of an emotionless face. I felt nothing. "Please, Lisa, please," he said.

I lifted my eyes slowly upwards and eventually met his eyes. "Hey, I am glad you are okay," he said. I nodded and looked quickly away. "Tonight is not the time to discuss this; you are half drunk and we are both really tired. We'll talk about this in the morning, okay? Is there anything you need right now?"

I thought for a minute. The morning was a horrifying thought. Tomorrow there would be no one left who loved me, Peter and his wife would be livid with me. I would be alone. "Are you mad at me?" I finally ask Peter.

"No. I am not mad at you," he answered.

"Will you be mad at me tomorrow?" I asked.

"No, I will not be mad at you tomorrow," he said again.

I was baffled, but too tired to inquire further. I just took that answer and reminded myself to breathe. Living each minute that night felt excruciating. Peter stood back up, motioned towards the guest room and asked again if there was anything I needed. I shook my head *no* and walked towards the bedroom.

An hour later I heard the door open and saw Peter's head pop in. I was sitting on the bed just staring into space. He was checking to make sure I was okay. We made eye contact and he asked, "Are you doing okay still?" I nodded and turned out the light to try to sleep.

The next day Peter wasn't angry with me. He later explained that he had made some bad decisions in his life also and needed people to give him grace and forgiveness. Those people didn't hold his actions against him. He explained that he planned to follow their example with this situation. He wasn't angry with me. And, he wasn't going to get angry with me.

He forgave me and to this day he and his wife have never held that night against me.

Chapter Four: Running Away

"Hey, Lisa!" I snapped back to the present moment as I heard a staff member call to me. I didn't bother to turn to around to see who it was. I was on a mission and I didn't want anyone to stop me. Shame, rage, and hopelessness pulsed through my body. I felt so ashamed to be labeled "Chemically Dependant."

"Lisa, wait up. Where are you going?" the staff member said. She caught up to me and was in my personal space bubble. I had no option but to stop or run into her.

"I just need to go," I said. "This doesn't matter anymore. This is entirely my fault. I am such a fuck-up. I deserve whatever happens to me." Tears threatened to well up and cascade down my cheeks.

"Lisa, look at me," Jessica said, the Eating Disorder Specialist from another residence hall. I looked up. I felt so broken, ugly, dirty and worthless.

"Tell me what's going on. Walk back to the residence hall with me," she said.

"Adelina met with me and told me I am 'Chemically Dependant.' That means there is no hope. I am a hopeless case," I said.

Jessica was shaking her head. "No," she said. "No. Lisa, there is always hope. You're here to get help."

A car drove by. Behind that car I saw the security van coming towards us to pick us up.

I had "code greened," which meant that I had tried to run away. It was an action that received much criticism from peers because of the disruption it caused. A number of staff from all over campus responded to every "code green" alert and went running to stop the person. It was usually a safety concern because the treatment center was responsible to maintain a level of accountability for residents' safety.

There was a resident last summer who ran away and made it to the railroad tracks. There was screaming as staff yelled over the walkie-talkies, "A train is coming!"

At the last moment the woman came off of the tracks and was brought safely back to campus. (And promptly sent to the hospital for a higher level of treatment care.)

There was another woman who jumped into the stagnant pond outside the residence hall to evade being caught. We all watched the action unfold out of the group room window. "Ew!" one woman exclaimed when they pulled the runner from the pond, "Turtles have sex in that pond!" We all laughed at the thought.

The day after I tried to walk off campus I found out that the car that drove by me and Jessica was one of my therapists. Her name was Moe. She said to me, "Lisa, I wish I would've known what was happening. I would have stopped and told you to get in the car. I would've said that we could go do whatever self-destructive thing you had planned but that you weren't going to do it alone."

I said, "Then I wouldn't have gone, if you were going with me."

Her words echoed in my mind and I felt loved. And validated. I imagined God would've said something similar to me. He would've said, "I'm going with you, Lisa. I am always with you. Even in your darkest moments."

Chapter Five: Vitals

It was 5:04am on a Tuesday morning. I heard someone calling my name, "Lisa. Lisa. Vitals today."

I mumbled, "Okay." And felt a thin fabric gown hit the blanket on top of my feet. I hated morning vitals. I was groggy from a medication change and exhausted from the intense day of groups yesterday. The last thing I wanted to do was roll out of bed, put on a gown, walk down the hall and stand in the line of ladies waiting to see the nurse.

God, I need you. I want to expect extraordinary things today. May my actions somehow glorify You. God help me believe in myself. Help me believe in You. Help me get through today making decisions that lean towards recovery and a more meaningful life.

My morning started every day with this prayer. It developed bit by bit as I picked up ideas of what I wanted to talk to God about and invite him into at the beginning of each day. Sometimes I found myself mumbling the prayer as I stumbled out of bed and started over because I wanted to be conscious of the words I was praying. I liked the prayer because it invited God into my day. It reminded me of what was most meaningful for me. And, it created a space for God to be with me in my day. Mornings were a super hard time of day for me.

Often praying this prayer and inviting a Power Greater than myself into my day was my bargaining chip with myself to agree to roll out of bed. I felt so anxious and overwhelmed in the morning. Usually I was just exiting the daze of a nightmare and had been up a lot during the night.

It was the middle of the summer and the low outside was almost 70-degrees. Inside it felt like 55-degrees, though. My body was malnourished and I couldn't keep warm; I was always cold. In 90-degree weather I would wear a sweatshirt and long pants between buildings on the treatment center campus.

I ran my fingers through my loose ponytail. A discouraging amount of hair came out of my head and stayed intertwined between my fingers. I hated that active eating disorders could cause my hair to fall out.

It was finally my turn to step into the room labeled "infirmary" where the nurse was waiting to take my vitals. The floor was tile and cold in there. I wrapped my arms around my body to try to keep warm.

"Sit down," the nurse said. Zarah was her name. She took my pulse and temperature. She asked me to put my arm forward so she could take my blood pressure. "Stand up," Zarah said. "Slowly," she added. I stood up, a bit overconfident. I had to work to hide how dizzied and weak I felt. "Okay, lets take your blood pressure again," Zarah said, as she put the stethoscope up to my arm and focused her attention on the blood pressure dial.

I had to have my blood pressure taken sitting down and standing up to see if I was orthostatic. Orthostasis was a possible medical complication of an eating disorder.

"Oh, you're not orthostatic anymore. We don't need to take your vitals standing up," the nurse said. I heard myself say, "Okay." And found myself thinking, *This obviously means that I don't have a 'real' eating disorder. It's not that bad. I'm actually probably fine and this is all an overreaction.*

Later in the day I found myself retelling the experience in an eating disorder process group. I told them how I had decided that no orthostasis meant no eating disorder. As I was talking I noticed my peers' reactions and took in what the therapist said. "Lisa, do you hear how ridiculous that sounds?" she asked.

"Yeah... I guess," I heard myself slowly mumble. Part of me was sure that this experience was evidence that I didn't even need treatment. I wasn't even orthostatic any more! And another part of me could see the therapist's point and laugh at how silly my rationalization and denial sounded.

"So, you like girls, right?" a woman said to me.

"No," I said.

"Really? I always just assumed that you did. I guess my gay-dar is off," she said.

It was not the first time that this conversation had happened and it didn't usually bother me. I didn't talk about intimate relationships or sex, mostly because neither were a big thing in my life right now. Part of me was grateful – I hadn't been married and divorced, I didn't have a sexually transmitted infection, and I was unscathed in some ways. And, I also felt a little left out. As if I was missing out on something. And I didn't want to miss out on something. Having sex was appealing in the fact that I hadn't had a lot of experience with it, but other than the allure of the unknown I had little desire to put a lot of effort into the issue. Plus, I was terrified that intimacy would bring up a lot of things from my past emotionally. I did want kids and I wanted to be married; I just wasn't in a rush to get there.

Chapter Six: Angels

"No!" I heard someone yell and was startled awake from a fitful sleep. I looked around the room in a groggy daze. I was the only one awake. I must've yelled in my sleep again. I was dreaming that a man was coming to hurt me and I couldn't get away. I just wanted him to kill me so that I could be out of my misery. My mind immediately connected the current terrified feeling to an unrelated terrified feeling in a childhood memory.

I couldn't sleep that night, once again. My parents were finally both home downstairs and I just wanted to be with them. Slowly I climbed out of my bed and walked quietly out my bedroom door. I tiptoed down the dark hallway. I stopped to listen at the top of the stairs. I could hear the TV on downstairs.

I knew that my dad was going to be angry that I was still awake and interrupting him. He was never happy to see me after I had been put to bed. I began to slide one step at a time down the stairs in my soft thin nightgown. As I neared the bottom of the stairs I peered through the banister, past the front door, and into the living room.

My parents were probably sitting on the couch farther back in the room than I could see. That's where I often found them. Sometimes, my mom would get up from the couch and walk towards me to put me back to bed. Other times, she would be held back by my dad's sharp words telling her to stop. He wanted me to go back up to bed on my own.

I inched forward a little more. As I turned the corner to announce my presence I saw only my dad on the couch. He didn't notice me at first, but his awareness of my company brought quick words, "Lisa, what are you doing up! Go back to bed."

His swift words were harsh and quietly pierced my sensitive heart. I contemplated returning to my room but paused to search the room with my eyes. *Where was my mom?* That was when I heard the soft muffled sounds of crying coming from the kitchen. I ignored my father's command and walked towards the kitchen.

Walking into the kitchen I saw my mom crumpled up on a chair with her head in her arms. A bolt of fear shot through my little body. Something was not right. My mom quickly noticed I was there and tried to hide the situation from me. "Hey honey, what are you doing up?" she said.

"Mom, are you okay? What happened?" I responded.

"Yeah, everything's fine. Your dad and I just had a fight. That's all," my mom tried to feign light-heartedness. Kids are perceptive, however, and I knew my mom wasn't telling the whole truth. I snuggled up next to her on the chair and we sat there for a few minutes. My dad was too angry to try to usher me upstairs.

Finally my mom spoke, "Come on, let's get you up to bed." We got up together and headed upstairs for the night. My little heart still felt full of confusion and fear.

I awoke to my mom shaking my shoulder. "Wake up, Lisa. Come on, we need to go," she urged me quietly and with urgency. It was the middle of the night. *Why in the world was my mom waking me up and where were we going?* I thought.

"Lisa, come on. I need you to wake up. Grab some clothes and your toothbrush," my mom reiterated her point.

I am awake. I am awake. I chanted to myself. I reached for the light and started getting my clothes in a pile. I was too groggy to make the situation feel anything but surreal.

My mom walked quickly back into the room. "Okay here is your toothbrush and your backpack. Throw everything in there. Grab your shoes and let's go," she said.

We drove a familiar route toward the grocery store. We turned and went past Arby's Restaurant and pulled into the parking lot behind a sign flashing "Motel" and "Vacancy."

I came back to the present. I noticed the feeling of my blanket on top of me and my mattress beneath me. My eyes slowly regained focus as my roommate at the treatment center opened our bedroom door. I remembered where I was and that I was safe. I sighed, relieved.

Sometimes lying in bed I would pray for God to help me get through this treatment center experience. A picture would appear in my mind of angels hovering above my room. I knew it sounded a little "out there." And, it was really comforting.

Angels made me think of my dog growing up. She was a collie and we had named her Angel. She was a miracle. My mom, my brother, and I loved that dog so much. She could bring the three of us together the way that nothing else could. She was literally an Angel in our midst.

I was in South Africa on a volunteer trip several summers ago. I worked for part of the time at an HIV/AIDS women's clinic. It was a bittersweet experience. I tangibly felt the preciousness of life. Men and women around me were positive with the HIV and AIDS virus. Women were deciding the fate of their unborn children.

The men and women who worked (paid and unpaid) at this clinic spoke during the morning meeting. Part of this morning meeting was a prayer time. Some staff talked about dreams that they had. They spoke of visions they had. They spoke of their intuition and of the Holy Spirit guiding them. In the States, where I am from, we do not give much heed to these things. Sitting in South Africa with the realities of life so close at hand, it seemed perfectly legitimate to interpret dreams, pray for healing, and expect that Holy Spirit to literally show up that day.

In this way I prayed and trusted that the angels who surrounded my bed at night were real. And that they were big and strong and would protect me and the other women I was with.

Chapter Seven: Run

Nadine was a fifty-one year old woman from the west coast. She was petite and thin from restricting. Her body language read "spunky." Her words indicated that she was a spitfire and ready to go. I liked her immediately. She was honest and stubborn and only spoke from a place of authenticity within her. She had been in and out of treatment for much of her life battling an eating disorder, and more recently, a narcotics addiction.

Nadine had endured things during her childhood years that were too much for an adult to endure. They were still very difficult for her to talk about. "My dad was a doctor," she said, "he was a podiatrist." We were in process group and Nadine had started to share. She went on to tell us how her father had decided to surgically alter her body once she had reached puberty. Obviously her father didn't have much expertise beyond feet. He ended up botching the surgery badly. Nadine's entire adult life she had carried these scars of shame and marring of her female sexuality.

Dr. Hailey said that this was considered sexual abuse. It was an extreme crossing of bodily boundaries. As Nadine told her story I was in awe of how strong she was. She had been through a lot and maintained so much resilience and dignity through it all. Sometimes I tried to sit next to her in hope that her awesomeness would seep onto me.

Nadine's story made me think about some of the times my boundaries were crossed and I was in scary situations growing up.

My mom had a few favorite phrases when she was really angry. They were "I hate you" and "I'm going to leave you and go on a long vacation!" She said them as if my brother and I were *the* overarching problem in her life. We were forces that were ruining her life.

In my mind I saw my mom's infuriated face: her jaw clenched, her hair wild, and her body tense. I saw her eyes open wide, staring intensely at me; they seemed so hard that I swore they could drill a hole through a brick wall. It scared the shit out of me. This was the face that would overtake my mom when she went into one of her blind rages. Rages that destroyed.

Before the rage ensued there was always a moment of realization that my mom's internal trip-wire had been triggered; there was a moment of calm before the rage. I recognized the calm and I knew instantly that I needed to look for a way out and run for it.

There were times that I would argue back to my mom and in response she would slap me. That enraged me; no one had the right to touch me. After being slapped one night by my mom I turned around hit her back. She had a look of disbelief on her face.

On my way out the door, running to avoid the blows, I knew I needed to grab everything valuable that was mine and take it with me. If anything was left out then there was a good chance it would end up broken. I couldn't even count how many telephones, remote controls, or dishes we went through on a regular basis. I had no idea how many holes were busted into the drywall, how many pieces of furniture were broken, or how many important things were cracked.

I remembered one time my brother and I got into a fight. I locked myself in my room, but my brother found my jewelry box lying around. It was a small wooden box with a glass window in the cover so that you could see into the box from the outside. He decided that to hurt me he was going to break my box. So he tried throwing it several times against the floor and against the wall. When that didn't work he found a hammer and began smashing the glass top to pieces. The shards scattered everywhere. I could hear him hammering from inside my locked room. There was nothing I could do except wait until my mom got home from work. It felt like chaos.

Another time that my brother and I got into a huge argument was the day before my first school baseball game. I had locked myself in the bathroom; it was the only door with a good lock. Before I got the bathroom door completely shut my brother had kicked it in. I had put my arm out to block the door from opening and felt a shot of pain go down my hand. I broke my index finger.

As my brother got older he got stronger. He didn't realize how strong he was. There came a time my senior year in high school when I had have to remove myself from my mom's house for my own safety. My brother would start yelling, "I am going to hurt you real bad this time, Lisa." There were times my mom pushed me out the garage door with the car keys because she had been afraid for my safety.

As was often the case, anything in the vicinity of my brother in a rage would be thrown in my direction. On one occasion the nearest thing was a kitchen bowl with a sharp knife in it. I watched my brother grab the knife and realized that I needed to run. At the same time in my head I thought, *He wouldn't really throw a knife at me, would he?* I was still under the illusion that there was some sense of sanity in our house. I bolted down the flight of stairs and turned the corner in time to hear a thud. When I turned around to see what had made the thud sound I saw what nearly missed me: the sharp kitchen knife was stuck into the floorboards. I looked up the flight of stairs to my brother and we locked eyes. It was a moment in slow motion. I slept in the parking lot in my car that night.

Sometimes when my mom or my brother got enraged I ran up to my room and hid in my closet corner. I always kept a shred of hope that they would forget I existed and I would be left out of the emotional tornado that was about to ensue. I wasn't usually that lucky. Sooner or later, I heard my mom's voice screaming my name from downstairs. Sometimes she stood right outside my room, piled all my belongings there, and just screamed at me.

"Why can't you pick up your shit? Why can't you and your brother just get along? You are going to drive me to the loony bin!!" she would say. The worst was when she would storm into my room and I was cornered. Her lips would be thin, her teeth would show, the muscles in her neck popped outward from her skin, and her voice was a full-out yell. "You and your brother are going to cause the police to come and you will have to go live with your dad. I am sure the neighbors can hear us. You are so selfish; why can't you think about anyone else?!" she would say.

My mom was a strong woman, too. If she decided to throw something or grabbed me by the arms I had to watch out, it was going to hurt. Sometimes she'd get so angry that she would leave in the car and came back hours later. One time my mom packed her suitcase and took it with her in the car. I really was concerned she wasn't coming back. Other times my mom would slam the door to her room and we'd see each other the next morning.

By the time morning came after a crazy night everything was magically great. There was probably breakfast made for us or we'd buy dinner out. My mom might come home with a little present for us of candy or some other trinket as a peace offering. There were confusing words spoken, "I'm so sorry. I made a mistake. I love you so much."

I used to call my mom from the cafeteria of my high school before classes started to make sure she wasn't still mad and that everything was okay; I didn't want to get hurt later.

After all of the apologies and peace offerings I felt so guilty. I felt guilty for saying things I shouldn't have said and doing things I shouldn't have done. I also felt guilty for feeling angry and hurt as a result of the actions of my mom or my brother.

The feelings of pain and anger didn't vanish with the two words "I'm sorry;" so was it wrong that I still felt angry and hurt? I felt guilty because I thought I had caused all of my mom's pain and was making her life more stressful. I felt guilty that I wasn't a better daughter, guilty that I didn't do more chores, and guilty that I felt guilty. It was ridiculous. If I talked about what happened to anyone outside of the family I also felt guilty. A pervading theme in our house became shame and guilt.

Several hours after an angry eruption, when everything was miraculously "great" again, I resisted accepting the façade my family put on. *Who were they kidding?* I thought. *Everything was still the same as it was five hours ago. I was still hurt and angry and frustrated. The same dysfunctions still existed in our family. There hadn't been any healthy conflict resolution. There were two new holes to cover up in the hallway and a broken piece of electronics to replace. Yet, we were back to one small happy family.* It was enough to make me crazy.

When I wouldn't accept playing along with this illusion my mom and my brother would get really upset with me. My brother would yell at me and say I was hurting my mom. He would tell me he didn't understand why I couldn't just forgive her, what had she done except try to give us anything we wanted. My mom would cry and cry and my brother would try to make her happy. I would get so frustrated. Beneath it all, I once again, felt like the entire situation was completely my fault. And, I felt very guilty.

After things at home had calmed down the scenario to repair the visible damage was pretty much the same. Tape the homework together. (What teacher would believe that my mom ripped it in a rage?) Fix the holes in the walls. Clean up the stuff thrown around. Get my things from the garage. And probably do extra cleaning and laundry to try to prevent another explosion.

I was so confused. How did I know when I could trust what someone says? How did I know which time to believe which things they said? How did I know who had an agenda and who didn't? How did I know what would cause an explosion and what would be okay? What happened when someone got mad? What did I do after that? I was so isolated trying to live covering things up and trying to prevent future episodes.

In elementary school I fell off of the wooden balance beam one day during recess. I fell face forward and slammed my chin into the beam. My jaw hurt so badly that it was all I could do to not cry. I refused to go to the nurse or even tell anyone how bad it was. I went the whole day without talking because it hurt to open my mouth to speak. No one noticed.

Growing up, change was closely associated with the feeling of pain. I learned early on to avoid all change. If that wasn't possible I learned to cover up all change. I resented, hid, and was afraid of maturing from childhood into being a young woman. I pretended to be ignorant or incapable of certain things so that my mom would feel useful and needed. Advice in relationships, feelings towards my father and his family, help with schoolwork, and even new vocabulary were all areas of growth that I hid from my mom. I felt devastated when I needed my first bra and got my first period.

Chapter Eight: Realizations

I was slowly accepting Adelina's diagnosis of Chemical Dependency. It terrified me at first. I searched for every reason why it could be not true. Slowly, I began to try on the label and see if it fit. I examined my life.

One morning I practically fell off of my chair with realization. I had a memory surface and with it I felt like I had been punched in the gut. The wind was knocked out of me.

Prior to coming to treatment I spent several days a week with one of the most beautiful little girls in the world. Her name was Lily. I was there in the hospital several hours after she was born. I took pride in the moment that she said my name (she called me "Sah" for awhile). I encouraged her to crawl and to walk. I spent Christmas and Thanksgiving with her and her family every year. I took her to the park and the zoo and to see the horses at a friend's barn. I took her to the children's museum and the lake and on errands. We bonded and I always thought that this might be the closest that I got to raising kids of my own.

Whether I could see myself having kids in the future or not, I took my relationship with Lily very seriously. I was intentionally present when I was spending time with her. I took pictures to document silly things we did. She went through a phase where everything was a cell phone. I have the cutest picture of her holding a banana up to her ear and pretending to talk to her grandma on it. We dyed Easter eggs and finger-painted and went on photography excursions (she used an old small digital camera I had and I used my newer nicer Canon SLR).

As I thought about a few of the times I had overdosed during the year before coming to treatment I had a horrible realization. I had put Lily at risk one morning without realizing it.

I had taken a bunch of medication the night before in an attempt to go to sleep and have a break from my anxiety. I woke up and drove to Lily's house. I wasn't feeling too well but pushed through with the normal activities all morning. We went and did errands. I felt increasingly dizzy and nauseous. We came home and I lay for the next several hours on the bathroom floor vomiting.

Lily sat with me playing with her baby dolls and trying to make me feel better. It turned out that I had taken a lot more prescription medication that I realized and was physically ill from it.

As I came to accept that I had a drug addiction, and the truth about this event, I was overcome with guilt and shame. As I processed these feelings I had a strong desire to be honest with Lily's parents. As I talked to Peter, her father, he said, "Lisa, I forgive you. I know that you will be that much more careful and attentive to our daughter in the future because of this. I know that you care deeply about Lily and would never do anything to intentionally put her in harms way."

I felt so relieved after this tearful conversation. It was still hard for me to love and accept myself knowing the danger I had put Lily in. With time I was able to accept it more fully. It helped to know that today I am choosing to live a sober healthy life. I am doing everything I can do never go back to those days of abusing medication and substances.

For three weeks I had been in room 203. It was down the first hallway and to the left, first door after the medication room.

It had a slight sour smell off and on during those three weeks. It smelled faintly like dirty socks, wet towels, or a stale drawer being opened.

One night I couldn't shake off the smell anymore; something really stunk. I opened all my drawers. I pulled out my laundry hamper. I went on a hunt for the cause of this sour smell. I traced it to the drawers under my bed. There was nothing in the drawers but folders and toiletries and note cards.

Then it dawned on me – the smell was *behind* the drawers. I don't know what sparked this thought. Perhaps my own sly sneaky side that unconsciously kept track of hiding places where my disease could thrive. I reached down below my bed and lifted the drawer off of its track. I pulled it forward and the smell wafted out and enveloped me. I gagged.

I saw two laundry detergent jugs under my bed.

They had been hidden ingeniously in the hollow space behind the drawer. They were jugs of old decomposing vomit. I turned away, covered my face with my arm and walked out of the room.

As I walked down the hallway I felt a mixture of things. I felt angry that there was disgusting puke under my bed and I had to sleep there tonight. I felt scared that these addictions and eating disorders could get to points where this was really happening. I felt sad that there was a girl who left here still actively purging in secret and who is really really ill. I felt sad remembering my own desperate moments.

The second day I was in treatment I had a compulsion that felt unstoppable. It was to vomit. I ended up puking in some towels in my closet. This was pretty desperate and humiliating.

I took a deep breath and continued looking for a MHC staff to support me in getting this situation taken care of.

Friday mornings were staff conference days. That meant that our whole treatment team (primary therapist, family therapist, dietitian, psychiatrist, and discharge planner) met in a group room in the residence hall and talked about us. Every other week we went into our staff conference to ask questions and hear feedback from the rest of the treatment team.

As one week turned into two and then three and then four I thought *I am almost done with treatment!* One week I asked, "What is my estimated length of stay?" I saw my primary therapist make eye contact with my family therapist. I expected them to say "two weeks" or something manageable. Instead, I heard them say, "Eight to ten more weeks." Tears welled up in my eyes and my chest tightened. *How is that possible?* I thought. *I thought I could do this and now I don't know.* My eyes shifted from looking at faces to looking at the floor. Eight to ten weeks felt like an eternity. *God, I can't do this on my own strength. I don't understand. And, I am really overwhelmed,* I prayed.

The core of healing and recovery lay in hope. A Power or Being greater than ourselves was vital to the existence of hope. At times I had made this Greater Being my therapist, my treatment team, Jesus or the collective group of my peers and their positive energy. If no Being existed that was greater than myself, then I was fucked. My best thinking and smartest ideas got me where I was. My greatest ideas about how to cope with life had landed me in life-threatening situations and in residential treatment.

My psychiatrist had a saying. She said that whatever we turned to when we were in crisis to solve our dilemma was our Higher Power. This caused great shame to rise within me. That meant that my eating disorder, self-injury, and drug addiction had been my Higher Powers.

I didn't grow up as a church-kid. In high school I had a friend who practically dragged me to her church youth group. The pastor stood up in front of the high school students and gave a short talk. "If you can convince me that I am wasting my life as a pastor," he said, "then I will gladly turn in my two-weeks notice and find a new life purpose."

Awesome! I thought. *A Christian who is reasonable! I will talk this pastor out of the existence of an invisible God, a book that is two thousand years old, and a person rising from the dead. This will be a piece of cake!*

Over the next ten months I read everything I could get my hands on – theology, philosophy, and biographies. I wrote down questions throughout the week and brought them to youth group and this pastor each weekend.

What happens to people who lived before Jesus was born? How can we prove Jesus rose from the dead? How do we know which translation of the Bible to read? How do we know there is a God? How do we know another religion or denomination doesn't have the 'right' way? How do we know that Jesus fulfills the Messianic prophecies of the Hebrew Old Testament? What about all the horrible things people do in God or Allah's name? What is grace? Why are people dying in famines and genocides? What did God let awful things happen to me when I was just a little innocent girl? How could God let my cousin die the way that he did?

I read Philip Yancey, Brennan Manning, Henri Nouwen, Lee Strobel, N.T. Wright, and C.S. Lewis. At the end of the year I came to a place where it made more sense intellectually to believe the basic tenants of the Church than to maintain a resistant stance. I still had questions, but the major building blocks were solid enough for me to start to build my life upon. I had experiences to indicate that there was a God and that he had been slowly and methodically revealing himself to humanity throughout history. Grace, redemption, and hope were key tenants of a life that authentically followed Jesus of Nazareth.

I grew in my faith and relationships with new friends who also desired to emulate the life of Jesus. As I did this the framework for the possibility to recover from the eating disorder and addictions in my life grew exponentially.

A Higher Power was an ever-evolving dynamic for humanity, both collectively and individually. Even those of us who had an identified God chosen, a spiritual community picked out, or preferred religion were constantly growing and learning and experiencing. In recovery we needed our Higher Power to be a loving, big, patient, honest, and gracious Being.

It was with similar skepticism that in my undergraduate studies I decided to major in Biblical Hebrew. I wanted to know how to "correctly" translate the Hebrew Old Testament. I wanted to know if Jesus really was the long ago predicted Messiah of the Hebrew Scriptures.

I approached all things the way my dad had taught me. Ever since I was little we would go on expeditions. My dad would do the research and we would drive to a piece of land in Southern Wisconsin. Once there, we would proceed to excavate. This involved prodding the river to see if we hit something hard that could possibly be a piece of pottery. We dug with shovels and searched with a metal detector for metal arrowheads. More often than not we didn't find anything, but sometimes we did. It was about the process of searching and the hope of finding something. We had the knowledge that there were artifacts to be found out there in Southern Wisconsin, it was just a matter of doing the research and finding them.

This was how I approached God and the Bible. I knew there was information about these things to be found, I just needed to find it. The search was worthwhile, no matter how long it took, because something valuable was out there to be found.

In the same way I searched for God and for artifacts, I came into contact with the twelve steps. I thought that they were another religion and unnecessary. However, the twelve steps were a core component of the treatment center's philosophy. There were twelve steps for every addiction – eating disorders, self-injury, sex and love addiction, alcohol and narcotic addiction, and even friends and family of addicts. When I was first introduced to the twelve step programs I hated them. I thought they were stupid and only for people who were desperate and really had a problem. I was wrong. They were a set of principles and actions immersed in a structure of community and support. They were not a punishment but rather an opportunity. In this way and as a result of hitting terrifying new bottoms I have cautiously embraced the twelve steps as a part of my recovery.

Chapter Nine:
Some Peace and Quiet

One of my friends from treatment was Allison. She was a twenty year old from Idaho with a similar set of challenges as myself. We had been together in treatment for going on twelve weeks.

One day we decided to go on a walk and be adventurous. We went to the pond with a jar and a laundry hamper. We had heard that the adolescents from another residence hall were allowed to have fish as pets. Allison and I intended to catch a tadpole and keep it as a pet. Of course none of this was officially condoned, but we were getting a bit antsy in residential treatment. Spring fever had caught up with us.

As we scooped water through the laundry hamper netting we brainstormed names for our little creature. Sam. Dani. Cory.

In the end we caught a minnow. We named it Cory because we didn't know how to determine the gender of a minnow. We got the official no-go to keep a minnow as a pet. Thankfully, our therapist agreed to keep Cory in his office in a jar for a few days before returning the little guy to the wild.

Chloe was an eighteen-year-old woman who had obviously been through hell and back. Or at least she was trying to come back. Her hair was an uneven short buzz cut. I came to find out later that her haircut was done impulsively one night with a pair of scissors shortly before she came to treatment.

Every time Chloe got uncomfortable, or group got too intense, she would start to say, "I'm a bumblebee. I'm a bumblebee." At first I thought it was strange and she was a little coo coo. With time, however, I discovered that she actually had some brilliant survival skills and was extremely bright.

Growing up, when Chloe's parents would fight and

violence would arise, she would maintain her mental safety by believing that she was a bumblebee.

Bumblebees don't get in the middle of arguments. Bumblebees don't take sides. Bumblebees don't cry or get hurt. A bumblebee can survive on its own. It allowed her to detach from traumatic and overwhelming situations and survive intact. Or mostly in tact, besides being in rehab.

Chloe was in my group at the treatment center. Her arms and legs were covered with scars. Pink and white lines covered her limbs. "Slut" was carved out on her left calf from one night long ago.

As we were sitting in group with Dr. Hailey, she began to share. "I never was girly," she said. "I was first molested by my step-father when I was five. That went on for six years. At sixteen, a boyfriend raped me. I never told anyone. I don't like to dress girly," she finished.

Dr. Hailey said, "Do you think your desire to hide your sexuality has anything to do with your sexual abuse?"

There was an awkward pause. "I guess so," Chloe replied.

"Do you wear girly clothing or style your hear in a

feminine way, though?" Dr. Hailey continued.

Chloe shook her head.

"Do you wear feminine colors? Like pink?"

"No. What do you mean…?" Chloe said. "I hate pink." Long pause. "My scars…? Is that what you mean? My scars are pink…?"

Dr. Hailey nodded and continued, "I want to see you wear pink somewhere besides your scars."

Dr. Hailey was the medical director of the treatment center. She was my doctor. She was incredible. Dr. Hailey was in recovery herself from several different things. She was patient, funny, and non-judgmental. She was very present during sessions and groups, both when conversation was happening and when silence was speaking. I had the feeling of being unalone. Sometimes that was the greatest gift I walked away with: the gift of being unalone in the midst of my pain.

Quite opposite to this experience was my stay at the hospital prior to coming to treatment.

I was on the adult acute inpatient psychiatric unit at a very well-respected hospital. The doctor sat in front of me and looked in my general direction. She asked, "How much of your meals are you finishing? How worried are you about gaining weight?" Her eyes were focused on some invisible wall between us. She was not present in the room with me. "Have you had urges to self-injure? Do you want anti-craving medication for your drug addiction?" she asked me.

In a very stressful situation a person who is currently active in an eating disorder, and receiving no accountability on their food intake (and absorption), the likelihood of unhealthy behaviors occurring is very high. This seems like an obvious observation to note. However, apparently it was not obvious to this doctor.

In the dining room I didn't take enough food to meet my meal plan. (A meal plan is a dietitian-prescribed food plan that will maintain a healthy body weight.) The doctor's question of "How much food off of your plate do you eat?" was irrelevant. Not to mention that the doctor failed to ask if I was skipping meals, eating the prescribed snacks, or purging after meals.

I mentally noted that I could get away with anything with this lady. Her one question (and the several questions that she failed to ask) indicated all this! I also mentally noted that this lady could not help with the eating disorder and tried to ignore the feeling of hopelessness that had begun to rise in my belly.

During this meeting with the doctor I started to wonder if my issues made me a freak. *If this doctor doesn't know the first thing about what I am struggling with then I must be extremely abnormal. Shit. She is obviously clueless,* I thought. *She doesn't even know enough to ask the right questions!*

Another time I decided to do the responsible thing and go see if I fucked up my body with my eating disorder relapse. I showed up at the hospital with the intention of seeing a medical doctor, getting labs drawn, and going home. Little did I realize that this visit to the hospital would leave me in a locked psych room and in the hands of the Emergency Mental Health Unit of the hospital.

It turned out that cases of eating disorders were seen as head-cases and if I was medically cleared then I had to also wait to be cleared by a psychiatrist. As 7pm April 16th turned to 4am and 1pm and 6pm April 17th, I was hydrated from the IVs, my fever had broken, and I was going stir crazy. (Warning: careful how you use the word "crazy" in situations such as this.) I was locked in a solitary white windowless "safe" room with my bed nailed to the floor. I guess not eating meant I was psychotic?

Hour 18 inside the little white room came and I had started to put fictional movie characters to the voices I heard passing by in the hallway. One guy was Yoda from Star Wars, I was sure of it. I imagined the two blue hospital gowns that I had on in opposite directions were a kimono or a Smurf costume. I had a new level of gratitude for how long that last five-percent of my phone battery actually lasted. And, the one good thing about that five-percent on my phone battery, which finally ran out: I didn't have to worry about talking to my dad again.

The first time I had tried to call him from the ER he was really angry. He said, "I can't believe you messed with your meal plan. You are not allowed to call me on my cell phone because it looks like you are trying to bypass my wife. You need to call our land line at the house, even though we don't answer it."

I said, "Okay, right, next time I'm out of the state in the emergency room and need to call you long distance I will be sure to call your landline that no one answers so that it doesn't look like I'm trying to just reach you. That makes perfect sense." My words were dripping with sarcasm. It took months to mend things between my dad and I after that episode.

Eventually, the hospital served me with a seven-page petition to keep me in the there for seventy-two hours. They claimed that by refusing to eat I was choosing die. It was a little bit true. I was passively choosing to die, but I thought it was ridiculous that I was legally forced to be in the psych ward when I was just trying to get my labs checked!

In the psych ward I did pretty well. One day, however, I refused to leave my room because I needed some alone time and the day room was chaotic. My anxiety was extremely high and the only quiet place I could find was my room. The staff took that as an indication that I was isolating and a red flag to possible self-destructive behaviors.

A staff member came in and without treating me like a human being he said, "I'm going to repeat myself three times. You need to get up and leave the room. You need to get up and leave the room. You need to get up and leave the room."

I sat in my bed because I am stubborn and I wasn't going to hurt myself, I just needed some peace and quiet! The staff member left and returned with three other staff members, all in latex gloves, and proceeded to pick me up off my bed and carry me down the hallway to the quiet room.

I was struggling to get free from this one lady's grip. Earlier in the day I had asked to use the bathroom. I had skipped lunch so there was no reason to monitor me in the bathroom – I had nothing to puke up! Despite this fact this lady was extremely rude and told me that I could not use the bathroom. Finally she said, "Well, I'm not the one with a problem of puking everything up, am I?" My jaw hung open. Did a professional really just say that to me? I was in shock. With her being significantly overweight what I should've said was, "No, obviously you have no problem keeping it all down and more!" But I was too stunned and hurt. Shame washed over me. And I had retreated to my room.

Now this awful lady was touching me (and I *hate* people touching me). I struggled to be free from her grasp. I was sure she was getting some sadistic pleasure out of the whole situation. The same staff member as before said, "Don't struggle; it will only make things worse. Don't struggle; it will only make things worse. Stop struggling; it will only make things worse." And then things got worse. I was grabbed even tighter and lifted off the floor until we reached the quiet room. It was awful.

The quiet room was a small, white, empty room, despite a nailed down bench of sorts, a one-way window to the staff area, and a door that locked from the outside. They forced me to sit down and told me that I had to stay there.

Under my breath I said, *Fuck you.* And I took my blankets and lay on the corner of this awful room and slept. At least it was quiet. It was the one place I could be by myself in this place and try to remember how to breathe again.

Three days later the petition to have me kept inpatient expired and I was released. The experience served as a reality check. And though it didn't feel like it, a reality check was definitely a positive thing.

Chapter Ten: Gourmet Dinner

I sat in front of a plate of tilapia and a salad at the lunch table. Mentally, I counted the calories of this meal. I added to that my last meal, my next meal, and my food yesterday. I tuned into how I felt in my body. *Do I feel fat? Are my clothes tight or touching me too much? Do I feel ugly or cute?* I factored that into my equation and decided if I could eat this meal without feeling guilty.

Surrounding me were eight other women staring at their trays with similar anxiety. Under the table my leg was bouncing up and down at a rapid pace, partially because I was cold and partially to release some of the internal anxiety.

I sat there trying to decide what would make this meal more edible. First, I decided that ketchup would help. I was not sure if it was normalized eating to put ketchup on fish, but it was a trick to get the food into my stomach. I grabbed seven packets from the cafeteria counter. We were only allowed two, but I knew that the staff at our table was new and probably didn't know that rule, nor would they realize condiment overuse was an eating disorder behavior (unless of course, they had gone through hell with this disease themselves).

Second, I decided that salt and pepper would help disguise my food and make it more edible. Sometimes disguising my food was a way to overcome my fears of eating a specific thing. And sometimes it was a way to make sure I didn't enjoy the food because that would make me feel guilty and afraid I might decide I liked food and eat uncontrollably. The eating disorder voice in my head screamed that I could not like food or desire food and needed to limit my food intake as much as possible. On my way past the ketchup bin I asked for salt and pepper packets, too. (We were only allowed two packets each of those, also.)

Third, I decided that making a stop by the soda machine was a good idea. Drinking soda water and diet soda would fill me up and mask some of the food with the artificial sweetener. We were only allowed one six-ounce glass of beverage besides water, but I filled up two glasses and bet that the staff would fail to notice this, also.

As I made my way back to my seat I inconspicuously looked at other ladies' trays and compared their lunch to mine. *Do I have the same amount as someone that I deem "normal weight" or "overweight"? Do I have less than someone who "truly" has an eating disorder and is skin-and-bones? Can I trust that my dietitian hasn't given me too big of a meal plan?*

As I walked past I saw plates with food cut up into tiny pieces no longer identifiable without close inspection. Ketchup and mustard lay on most trays with unusual combinations. Salt and pepper was sprinkled over everything. Glasses of diet soda sat next to trays like garnish on a fancy dinner. Even though diet beverages weren't allowed, while regular calorie soda was, the appearance of regular and diet soda was indistinguishable and therefore it was an honesty system. We took full advantage of that system.

I saw napkins quickly hide food from trays and

disappear into laps with silent prayers from ladies betraying their desire to recover. I saw cans of nutritional supplements dotting some tables according to who was struggling with their meal. I heard group games of "Twenty Questions," "Guess the Celebrity," and word games bouncing around the meal tables with a hollow desperation. If only they would distract us from the food we were eating long enough to get it into our mouths. If only the games could distract us enough to drown out the eating disorder voice in our minds that talked at us unceasingly.

I sat back down to the table and my tray. I methodically doused my food with condiments. I cut the fish into tiny squares and the cucumbers in my salad into quarters. I took a bite and followed it closely with diet soda, holding my breath all the while. Finally, like a punctured bike tire, I let my breath out and relaxed my shoulders. One bite down.

As I ate the tilapia fish and the tossed salad for lunch I was immediately brought back to my childhood. Besides the times when I was volunteering abroad and *had* to eat fish I hadn't *chosen* to eat fish in more than fifteen years. I was brought back to frozen and breaded fish sticks that my mom made when I was little. I saw our old house with the blue and white speckled kitchen walls. I saw my brother and I sitting at the table with our plastic kid-plates in front of us. I felt the anxiety pulse through my body.

My anxiety stemmed from growing up in chronic fight-or-flight situations. The first eighteen years of my life trained me to be anxious, on alert, jumpy, and ready for anything at any time. I learned to be guarded with other people. I learned to not trust and to be suspicious of others' motives. I learned to test the water, so to speak, to see if it was safe. I tested it over and over and over before jumping in. I learned that where I was going to sleep the next night, or if I will awaken in the middle of the night to a chaotic situation, was always up to chance. I learned that peoples' love, moods, attention, boundaries, sobriety, and presence was never consistent.

My parents were fighting, again. "LISA! Clean this shit up!"

Why was I getting screamed at just because my parents were having a disagreement? I thought.

"Take your brother and go upstairs when you are done," my mom said.

It was everything I could do to keep the hot tears of hurt from streaming down my cheeks. I got up and stepped towards the TV to shut it off, glancing at the same time towards my dad heading out the garage door. I wondered when he would come home again. I could hear my mom slamming pots and dishes in the kitchen. My little brother stood motionless next to me staring at my mom.

"Come on, buddy," I said, using everything inside of me to keep my voice from trembling, "Lets go upstairs." We quickly walked in step up the stairs and split when we reach the top. We each went to our separate rooms; we wanted to be alone to process our feelings.

My heart felt so heavy and I felt so sad. I retreated to my safe place. Taking all the blankets off of my bed I headed towards my bedroom closet and I crawled as far back into the corner as I could. I covered my head with the blankets and let myself cry. The sobs came out in a sound that felt ugly. I had been holding it in for too long and all of the emotion began to pour out. I screamed into my blanket and used the bedding to muffle the sound of my pain. I felt so angry.

It would be better if I had never been born. I am bad and there is no one who loves me. I wish I was dead. I wish I was dead, I thought. I wrapped myself up tighter in my blankets and moved closer into the corner of my closet. My little hands balled up into clenched fists and I squeezed my eyes tightly shut. *It's going to be okay. I wish I had never been born.*

Sometimes my mom quieted down from her rage and came to find me curled up in the closet. She pushed the hanging clothes to the side and bent down to be eye-level with my jumble of blankets. In between child-sized sobs I exhaled the painful confession that I should never have been born, "There is no one who loves me. I am not worth loving. I only do bad things that cause you and dad to hurt."

She countered my thoughts and told me that I was loved, "Your grandma and grandpa love you. I love you. Your dad and your brother love you. Your best friend loves you. Your aunt and your uncle love you."

A seed of despair and hopelessness was planted. The people my mother listed off didn't know me and they didn't know what was going on inside my home. They didn't invest in my life, spend time with me, talk to me, listen to me, or know the names of my friends. Their love didn't make me feel lovable, like I belonged, confident, unashamed, safe, or whole. It all felt empty.

My desire for a family, my need for a place to belong, and my longing for a home I felt safe in was far from sated. *Were these things I really needed or were they merely wishful thinking? Maybe only lovable and deserving kids got these things.* I thought.

My blankets were soaked with tears by now. My mom didn't come in to find me. I cried myself to sleep. When I woke an hour later I told myself that everything was going to be okay; everything was going to be okay. And I tried to believe it.

Most memories that flooded back from the past were scary or anxiety-ridden. At random times I would be triggered to remember something from the past. A smell or taste or feeling in the air could trigger a memory. It meant that I was constantly on guard and waiting for the next thing to come upon me unexpectedly.

This excruciating lunch process continued for twenty-five more minutes until the end of the time allotted for meals. I heard staff say, "We're at the time-boundary, ladies. Does anyone need an Ensure before we F.A.F.?" One lady nodded and went up to the cafeteria line to get the nutrition supplement so that she could "complete" her meal. She knew that if she failed to finish the food on her plate, or the caloric equivalent with Ensure, that it would be marked as "incomplete" and counted as restricting.

F.A.F. stood for Food And Feelings. At the end of every meal we did it to help connect our food-life with our feelings behind it. We went in a circle and each person answered a few questions: How was your food? How full do you feel physically? How do you feel emotionally? We saved comments about the food, weight, exercise, body image, and any other topic remotely connected to eating disorders until after we had finished the meal. Failure to do this could result in a peer harshly correcting you. The meal support tables were tense and emotions often ran high.

As we finished the F.A.F. the staff went to each lady and checked under every plate and bowl, uncrumpled every napkin, and patted down everyone's pockets before we were cleared to take our trays to the dishwasher. The staff charted how much of our meals we had completed.

Those of us medically stable enough to walk back to the residence hall started on our way. And those of us with a weight that was too low or electrolytes that were too unbalanced waited for the security driver to come and pick us up to take us the several hundred yards to our residence hall.

I sighed. Meal number two done for the day. Only two snacks, one meal, and four groups left until I could go to bed.

Chapter Eleven: Support

"I don't want to enable you," my dad said. "So we have decided not to financially support you when you leave treatment this time. We will help with your insurance premium for six months and that's it." As my dad finished talking my heart sunk. He thought eating disorders were the same as drug addictions and that recovery was a decision of willpower.

Though they were both addictions – one a physical addiction and one an emotional process addiction, there were fundamental differences. An eating disorder must be treated with the very substance that is the addiction. It was similar to telling an alcoholic, "Listen, you must have three beers a day. No more and no less. Now go and recover." It was tricky and required trial and error and a lot of support.

I was not back in treatment because I had been fucking around. I had two sponsors. I got *myself* back to treatment. I made and continued to make choices towards life. Supporting that would have been supporting *recovery*. Not to mention that I had recently started taking hardcore mood stabilizing drugs per the indication that I was likely Bipolar Type II. Not being on the right medications and being Bipolar was an extremely difficult (if not nearly impossible) endeavor. It made me feel ashamed and frustrated and worthless when my dad treated me like this. *What the fuck*, I thought. *If only he knew what depths the depression got to at times, then would he be a more supportive father?*

The night was tumbling forward. Things on a downhill spiral had been lethargically happening the past week. It was nearly impossible to get out of bed; an awaiting day conjured up feelings of dread and fear at the impossible task. How it was that I did life everyday up until then I was at a loss to recall. I'd been seriously entertaining the idea of suicide for weeks by now. Everything seemed to stab pain into my life. There didn't seem to be hope for change. There was nowhere to go.

I grabbed the bottle of pills I had planned to take and walked out of my dorm room. If I overdosed I would either die and end all this or get help, right? It was a win-win situation.

I sat in the concrete dirty stairwell with my dorm key, water bottle, bottle of pills, and my cell phone. Maybe God would miraculously intervene with someone calling me? I counted out pills and started taking them one by one. One. Two. Three. Four. *Should I call someone? Was it bad enough? Would it be okay? They might get angry if I didn't.* So I dialed my friend's number. I left a message. *Well, I tried, if he didn't call back soon, it wouldn't matter anyways. I could always walk to the emergency room before I died.* I sat there and tried to think clearly. *How did I get here? What do I need to do this? I could stop now. But what's the alternative? It'll happen eventually. How will things get better?* The phone rang. It was my friend. *I could not answer it,* I thought. Relief, dread, and regret washed over me at once. *Was I betraying myself – my deepest feelings and intentions? I was being a traitor to myself.* In an instant of bravery I push the button under "answer."

"Hello?" I stammered in a surprised innocent voice. I was attempting to cover up the fear and pain I felt. *Could he tell anyways?* I wondered.

"Hey, what's up?" My friend responded in his southern-accent tinged voice. I shouldn't have called. He was busy. I couldn't back out now. "Nothing." I tried to buy time. I couldn't say it. I couldn't say *I'm sitting here holding ten extra-strength Tylenol in my hand and I already took four.* I didn't know where to start or how to speak.

"Really? I don't think that's why you called. How's your night going?" It was after eleven at night. I was shaky and on edge. Reality seemed hard to keep concrete. Every time my friend's voice transversed the invisible gap between us it surprised me and pulled me slightly up from the rapids of stuttering dumfounded thought that I was attempting to control inside my head.

"Not so good." I responded. He knew me too well to let that slide. He pressed further and tried to evaluate the situation, "How so?"

"I don't know," I replied. "I'm just having a bad night," I continued, stating the obvious.

"What'd you do today?" My friend pressed further.

With tears nearly in my eyes I heard myself say, "I just want to die... really bad." I blurted it out. It was my cry for help from so deep inside. I didn't know how to word it more descriptively. Or explain it more aptly. He proceeded to talk and tried to change my perspective; tried to find things I could do to "fix" this situation.

This time none of it helped. Things were hurting too deeply; the level of this night was too imbedded in hopelessness for the average half-hour band-aid answer. The pills were sweaty in my hand. The red was transferring to my palm. He had no idea that I was crouched in the corner of a stone dormitory stairwell holding pills and on the phone with him as my only line to hope. I knew he had worked all day already, he was beat and I could hear the tiredness in his voice. I heard the TV on in the background. I was sure that everything in him wanted to not call me back, to watch TV, take a shower, and go to bed. I felt guilty.

After he stopped talking, I just sat there silently. He was realizing that the band-aid thirty-minute talk wasn't working tonight. The 'rationalize things and tomorrow will be better' talk.

"You realize, that if you were talking to anyone else, they would tell you to go to a hospital, don't you?" he asked.

"...okay." I answered. What did that matter, if he was not telling me to do that? What did that matter, if he knew I wouldn't go to the hospital? What did that matter, if that was exactly *why* I didn't call a therapist or crisis line? It would take away any control that I had. I would cease to be a person, just a crisis and liability.

I heard my friend sigh. I had reached his limit. He was out of answers, quick fixes; he was out of ideas.

"Lisa, I don't have anything else to tell you. Can't you just go take a shower and go to bed?" I could tell he had wanted to end the conversation a long time ago. He must have realized that I felt especially desperate tonight.

"I don't know," I responded. He sat there and tried to grasp at anything to understand or help. He was confused and dumbfounded. There were no categories for how to deal with this kind of situation. There were no ways to make him understand. I didn't have words or reasons to tell him in a way that made sense.

Eventually, I did begin to feel tired. I felt less alone and desperate – at least someone else knew exactly where I was at and was walking with me trying to fight this battle to choose life. The next time he asked if I could just take a shower and go to bed I agreed. "It's almost one in the morning, you must be getting tired," my friend stated. I hadn't realized how much time had passed. We had been on the phone quite a while.

It gave me just enough courage and hope that I got up off the floor, walked to my room, and put myself to bed.

"Sometimes I feel sad that my main support system isn't my biological family," I said. I was talking to a MHC named Yeonella. She was a staff member that I looked up to a great deal. She was in her late twenties, a few years older than I was. I knew that she had been a resident at another treatment center in another part of the country when she was younger.

"I understand what you mean," Yeonella said. She had grown up with a family that had a similar lack of support. "Growing up I always pictured myself as an old piece of meat left in the back of the fridge: forgotten, old, moldy, and unwanted."

"Yeah! That's a perfect image for how it feels to be left behind," I said.

Chapter Twelve: Mistakes

As I walked back to the residence hall at the treatment center I saw three police cars pulled up out front. *That's odd,* I thought. *Usually if something happened they called a private ambulance company to transfer someone to the hospital.*

I walked into the hall and came to find out that this is what happened. MaryLou had been on the phone. She had been dialing and pushed nine on the number pad to get out of the phone system of the treatment center. Then she had pushed one to begin to dial a long-distance number. At that point she had reached over to answer the phone next to her.

"Hello," she said. Meanwhile, in reaching over to

the next phone she bumped the number one again on her own number pad.

"Hello? Can I help you?" the nine-one-one operator came on the line.

Silence. There was silence because MaryLou was still taking a message on the phone next to her. She then hung up her phone (thinking she hadn't dialed anyone) to go to find the person for the phone next to her. MaryLou's phone rang and another lady named Rachel answered.

"Hello?"

"Hi, this is the nine-one-one operator. Can you tell me where you are calling from?" she asked.

Rachel panicked and didn't know what to do. We are not allowed to give out information about where we are calling from because of confidentiality. Rachel finally said, "No."

"Can you tell me your name?" the operator asked.

"No," said Rachel, for similar reasons.

The operator asked again, "Is there an emergency? Can you tell me where you're calling from?"

"No," she answered.

According to protocol, the vague answers necessitated the police coming to do a wellness check.

Hence, the police cars had shown up and wanted to question the callers. It was pretty funny once we figured out how the mishap had occurred.

I was at a weekly meeting with my family therapist. We had been conference calling with my dad, my mom, and my dad's wife, Dawn.

"What kind of flashbacks do you have?! Why can't you just move on with your life? Just think about the future." My dad said. He was always full of advice that I hadn't asked for and ideas on how I could live my life. I immediately felt ashamed and worthless; obviously I was failing at life.

My family therapist responded, "Lisa, do you think that you would be willing to share with everyone what some of your flashbacks are?"

I nodded, *Yes*. I stretched and twisted and contorted a hair band in my fingers. Very quietly I said, "Yes. I have memories of being sexually abused…"

Immediately my mother responded, "What?! Did I just hear you say 'sexually abused'? That did not happen. That *did not* happen."

I heard my dad cut her off, "Wait a minute. Are you

telling me that you people at the treatment center are actually entertaining the possibility that this is true? There is no way that this actually happened."

"This is ridiculous," my mom's voice chimed in again.

I sat in the chair at the treatment center staring blankly in the direction of the phone and the voices of my family in another state. My legs were curled up tight next to my chest and my arms wrapped limply around them. In my left hand I was still holding the hair tie that I had been playing with. My family therapist Piper sat in front of me and to the left a little. Her elbows were resting on her knees and she leaned forward. Her face was focused on me and I could tell that she was reading my body language.

"Lisa," she whispered. "Lisa." There was a cacophony of my mom and dad's voices coming out of the phone in between us. I slowly registered that Piper was calling my name and came back from a far away place in my mind. I focused on her eyes and silently asked, *What?* My attention was divided. Much of it was lost in a far away place in my mind. It was a place in my mind where I felt safe.

I heard Piper edge her way into the voices, "I just

wanted to check in with Lisa because I know this is a really hard thing for her to talk about."

I heard my dad's wife come through the wires. She had been silent until now (probably because it would have been impossible to get a word in edgewise).

"I know this is probably a really hard conversation for everyone to have," she said. "I'm at an advantage because I am a little bit removed from the situation by being a step-parent and not blood related." A flicker of gratitude for Dawn passed through my heart.

I heard my mom's voice jump back onto the line, "What are we supposed to do when you tell us this kind of information? This did not happen."

I went to the far away safe place in my mind again. My eyes glazed over. Two thoughts dominated my mind, "I want to run away" and "I want to hurt myself." I stood up and moved towards the door as the angry voices continued to come out of the speaker on the phone. They were invalidating voices and ones that pricked my heart. I felt so ashamed and disappointed and afraid. Piper was following me with her eyes. "Wait, Lisa," she whispered.

No, I shook my head. I left the small session room and walked towards the residence hall exit. *I can't do this. This is too much,* I thought. *I just need to cut myself.*

I found a MHC. "Can you let me out?" I asked.

The MHC was a bit distracted and didn't realize that I was extremely upset. She let me out and I promptly walked towards the campus exit. *I just need to buy a legitimate razor and hurt myself and buy a diet soda. Then I will be okay,* I thought. A staff member saw me walking and could tell immediately that I was extremely upset. I felt like I was suffocating and needed a breath of air. We talked for a few minutes and she supported me to be able to go back to the residence hall.

I felt distraught and despair as I sat on my bed. I sobbed and cried out to God. *I feel so alone. God, how could you let my family session go like that? Why did you give me a family that is unable to love me? Why did you let horrible things happen to me when I was too little to know better? Do you even love me? Are you even here?*

Running away was an understandable reaction. And when thought about, it made perfect sense. I chose an eating disorder or self-harm or substances to get a break from my anxiety and my troubles. I "ran away" every time I used or restricted or purged. It made perfect sense that I would continue to try to run away – physically, literally, and through food or sex or substances – because that was what I knew. It was a path that I knew. And when I was in crisis, like all humans, I went to what I knew as my first reaction. After some time – seconds or minutes or hours or days, I could slow down and go to new coping skills. And, this took time to learn. It took a lot of trial and error.

I showed up one time to a PHP (partial hospitalization program) and had a really intense panic attack. I used the classic line: "I need to go get something from my car." And bolted from the building. I went home and took a nap and tried to remember how to breathe.

From my perspective it was a crisis and there was no one safe for me to talk to because it was a totally new environment. I was doing what I thought I needed to in order to survive.

From the perspective of the staff at the PHP program I was irresponsible, I didn't take treatment seriously, and I was really frustrating. *How could she just leave?* They asked. They didn't understand how I could just disappear and think that was okay.

And, disappearing had been my mode of operation

for years. Physically disappearing by not eating, relationally disappearing by pushing people away, and letting my life disappear by throwing it away using and self-harming and so on.

That's what we who are addicts (to eating disorders, self-harm, and substances) are best at – disappearing and running away! It should be no shock to health care professionals or loved ones when someone who is sick runs away, metaphorically or literally. It's part of the disease. And when we run we're just trying to do what we know will help us survive. It *does not* mean we are not invested in treatment or that we are trying to be irresponsible or put a wrench in the plans. It *does* mean that we have a life-threatening illness (maybe more than one) and that it is really serious; it is causing us to wreak havoc and destroy all areas of our lives.

I felt the allure, the pull, the craving for darkness. It beckoned me to a place where there was no light to see myself and feel the shame. It told me of a place where things didn't hurt, where I set my standards so low that I would never be disappointed. Where I could finally lay down my weary body to sleep. The cheap adrenaline of the spiral descent farther and farther down into hell (addiction, depression, alcohol, pills, self-injury, and suicide) was so appealing. This descent was so tangible that I could feel it like goose bumps on my skin. It was so real that I was afraid to whisper it out loud, lest I wake myself and discover this was where I was.

I had heard of another place, a place where things were different. They told me it was a place where fear didn't reign, pain didn't define, and feelings didn't last forever. I heard it was a place where I would love myself and see myself as worthy. People said it was a place where love was real, hope could be touched, and we weren't alone in life. I had heard people have deep relationships, got their needs met, and had energy to feel joy.

I was told the journey from the prison of darkness to the freedom of hope was through treacherous terrain. There were steep mountains where things got harder, colder, scarier, and more demanding before they got better. The mountain passes were tight and required letting go of all the baggage a traveler attempted to bring through. The wind was fierce and required transparency to let the shame, pride, and anger be stripped away. The journey was long, much too long for any person to do alone. It required asking for help and allowing others to walk next to us along the way. The path through was dangerous, lined with tragedies, traumas, and traps, all which forced us to confront our deepest fears head-on.

I was told this journey was the one worth taking, offering the most hope and fulfillment. I was told that this journey really was possible to survive, even if the place I was currently in had the hollow remains all around of those who had tried and failed or failed to try at all.

I thought that I wanted to try that life; I wanted to be adventurous, go forth with courage, and choose to believe there really was another way. Sometimes, however, my strength wavered, my courage failed, and my shame pulled me off the cliff to tumble down to the rocks below. I didn't know how many times I could get up and convince myself to try again. I didn't know if I was strong enough to fight long enough – without rest, without comfort and feeling great pain – to make it any significant distance to this place I had been told exists.

God give me the strength to live through this hour and not call out to my friends-of-darkness to make me un-alone. I cried out to God.

Later in the afternoon of my awful family therapy session, my family therapist Piper came to talk to me. "Hey Lisa," she said as she stuck her head in my bedroom door.

"Hi," I answered. I was miserable and extremely discouraged, to say the least.

"I was wondering if you would be available to talk for a minute."

Yeah, I nodded and walked out into the hallway.

"I want to tell you a story… and I am not sure if it will make sense… but I keep thinking about it when I am with you and I think it could help."

Yeah. Okay, I nodded my head again and made eye contact. I was just grateful someone from my treatment team was coming to talk to me and had sought me out. I needed someone to love on me because the family therapy session was like bomb exploded on the surface of my heart. Now all that was left was a desolation and a huge crater craving to be whole.

"I want to tell you about a girl I met at a place I used to work." Piper continued, "She was at a facility a little bit different than this one. Every so often she would have a tantrum and refuse to go to the dining hall. We would order her food down to the unit and she would still have a huge breakdown on unit. We couldn't figure out what was going on. It went on for a long time. Some staff were frustrated and some of us were curious.

"We started to keep track of which days she had an episode. Every time that peas and carrots were served on the menu this girl would have an outburst. Once we noticed the pattern we could count on her reaction and change the experience. We would have her meal called down and make sure there were no peas or carrots on her tray.

"As we investigated the meaning behind the peas and carrots we hit upon something really important. When this girl was younger and would spend time at her grandparents' house her grandma would always cook peas and carrots. She was molested in the living room by her grandfather while her grandma cooked dinner. The peas and carrots triggered memories of being molested.

"I wanted to tell you that it's okay if it's not what it looks like on the surface. It looked like peas and carrots were what made this girl upset. But it was about so much more than peas and carrots. When we took the time to talk to the girl and really partner with her in finding out what was going on we discovered the legitimate reason for her panic.

"I want to tell you that sometimes it's more than just peas and carrots. It makes sense that you have gone through the things you have gone through. Don't let your family tell you it's just peas and carrots if it's not. It makes sense that your memories and flashbacks are pointing towards more than just peas and carrots. Trust yourself. Trust your memories."

A feeling of gratitude welled up in my chest. It was hard enough for me to talk about my memories out loud, but to have my family invalidate them felt unbearable. The rest of the day I just kept repeating to myself: *It's more than just peas and carrots, it's more than just peas and carrots. And that's okay. I am not crazy. Sometimes it is more than just peas and carrots.*

I was at an S.M.A. meeting on a Sunday night. S.M.A. stood for "Self-Mutilators Anonymous," an attempt to apply the twelve steps to the issue of self-injury. The lady leading it was doing her very best. She sat with her hair cut in an uneven short crop. (It had been cut with nail clippers.) She was nervous and wore a scarf over her head. She unconsciously repeatedly pulled out her hair, piece by piece. I was irritable after a long day already. A meeting leader with Trichotillomania self-injuring right in front of me was the last straw. I tuned out the meeting and pulled out a crossword.

Self-injury had been a part of my story for nine years now. I had journals full of entries about self-injury.

The cutting was bad tonight. It had been so long since I used my favorite spot. Over and over and over again I cut until the skin glistened with blood. As if it was sweating. Tape it shut, it shouldn't be too bad. One cut spurted. That was interesting. It was always a game – how far could I push on this part of skin with this razor? How deep could I go? How far could I push that fear back? I finally stopped the relentless act; I'd been at it over an hour. As time went on, my cutting got deeper and deeper, and the funny thing was, I felt less and less pain. I would cut, see it was pretty deep, and put the Kleenex on it to catch the dripping blood, but feel absolutely nothing. Maybe it was time to stop. There was a Monster inside of me. The Monster was terrified of everything and always beating me with a hammer. It drowned out good and God, hope, peace, love, confidence, and reason. The sadness, guilt, fear, and anxiety hung in the air like the humidity on a night dripping with moisture. It was just easier and more comfortable to be alone, or with someone who understood. It was not that I didn't want friends, or to push myself to change, it was that I couldn't take the next step unless this Monster inside of me was a little bit quieter. The only way I knew to quiet the Monster was to cut myself. So I did. When I was done I packed up the first-aid bag and razors for the next time. I brushed my teeth. Read a book. At least I was able to do these things now. Now that I was calm. And I could fall asleep so easily. Sleep could come now. The worry and fear, anxiety, tension, and Monster inside were all a little quieter. Maybe it would be okay. Maybe it would be okay.

There's a story in the New Testament that speaks about a man who cuts himself. It is in Mark 5:1-20. Even though it seemed like everyone else had given up on the man, Jesus was not deterred. He went right up and healed the man. Afterwards, it says that the man "was sitting there, dressed and in his right mind." I love that this story is in the Bible and that Jesus himself met a person suffering with this very problem of self-injury. I had proof that Jesus would respond with mercy and heal me, if only I would come to Him. The healing may not be over night or in my timeframe, but it would surely come. Jesus did not see someone who cut him or herself as beyond hope or too far gone. He did not see someone who cut him or herself as crazy or worthless. He approached him and he healed him. I prayed that as I approached Jesus he would heal me, also.

Chapter Thirteen: Anger

Once a week we exchanged snaps with each other in the residence hall. If someone had done something great that was noticed then she could be given a snap by one of her peers. We wrote them on small pieces of paper and put them in our "SNAPS" box. Sometimes snaps said, "You did great in process group" or "You did great with your meals." Other times snaps were encouragement regarding recovery in general, "You deserve a meaningful life" or "You are not alone and we believe in you."

One week a disturbing snap surfaced. "You should've killed yourself," it said. We had an emergency residence hall meeting the following day.

The snap was intended for a woman named Sarah. Sarah was a middle-aged woman from Florida. She was overweight and had scars and cuts up and down her arms. I got this weird vibe from Sarah. The entire residence hall meeting was spent pointing fingers and admonishing the writer of the anonymous note. *I'm skeptical,* I thought. *Something weird is going on with this note.*

It turned out that Sarah had written the note to herself. I was livid. She claimed that she was dissociated and wrote the note and didn't remember. I thought, *This is fucking bullshit.*

During group later in the week Sarah said, "I don't know why people don't believe what I say." I couldn't hold it in anymore. I said, "Because you write notes to yourself and then lie about it!!" Something about the situation didn't feel right; it felt bogus. I felt disrespected. And I was tired of listening to the bullshit.

I found out the next night that a woman whom I had been in treatment with passed away. This was the third lady I knew that had died this summer. I was sure that part of the reason why the number was at three was the amount of time I had spent in treatment over the past two years; I met so many women. And part of it was the craftiness of these diseases.

Eating disorders, substance addictions, and mental illness are diseases that are increasingly serious as they progress and they are deadly in nature. They don't mess around. They don't always give second or third or fourth chances.

The longer I was around recovery communities the more I was going to know women who succumbed to their diseases, as well as women who had successful recoveries. It shouldn't have shocked me that people I knew were dying; most of us had tried to commit suicide at some point or another. The chances were high that of those of us that relapsed most would put ourselves in life-threatening situations again.

As I talked to my chosen-family (a group of friends who functioned for me as a family might) back home I told them about the death I had learned about. I expressed my frustration and anger. I honored that part of me that was jealous of the fact that this lady was now done fighting her battle; she could finally rest. I still had to fight for recovery and fight for life. With that said I was livid that another woman whom I had known had died from these diseases. I was terrified because I was fighting the same diseases that killed these three women this summer.

"We need you," Peter said. "You are not going to die from this. Our family needs you. I'm really sorry to hear about your friend."

"Yeah. It's okay. I am just upset," I said. Peter's words comforted me. I knew he had no way of knowing if I was going to be among those who recovered and died of natural causes, but his support was standard for my chosen-family. They were determined to stand with me and support me through these battles. They spoke with loving candor to me when I didn't want to hear what they were saying. They communicated with each other and held me accountable. They continually were involved in my life and treatment and spoke truth to me. They were all people from my church, the one I got connected with in high school. They would tell me that I was loved by people and by God, that grace was a real and tangible thing, and that there was hope.

The foundation of the gospel was that Christ had come, He had died, and he had risen again. In this way we could now have a restored relationship with God, with ourselves, with nature, and with each other. This meant that although the world was still broken, it and we were in the process of being restored and redeemed day by day. One day, all things would be made right. All who desired to be with God would be with Him. And those who didn't want to be with God – well, He's a gentleman, so they say – and He won't force anybody.

That's where one misconception often popped up. Hell is horrible because it is a place that lacks everything that God embodies: love, joy, wholeness, grace, hope, relationships, and beauty. If someone doesn't want to be with God and they choose "hell" it is their choice, but it is not a punishment. I want to be around those things: joy, wholeness, peace, love, and beauty; I want to be with God, whoever He is. My idea of Him grows and blossoms and evolves all the time. Yeah, the fundamental characteristics of him are fixed: He is gracious, He is omnipresent, He is more powerful than death, He embodies perfect love, but there is so much else that He is! And it is a joy to discover that each and everyday.

I wrote an email to Ben after receiving the news of the death of my peer. I said: *I don't want to die from theses diseases or suicide. I want my tombstone to say: died of old age.*

As I was reading I stumbled across an idea that I

loved. I knew I wanted a tattoo. I knew I wanted it to say something about living and being loved. I wanted it to be a statement to myself about how I am choosing to live my life. The protagonist in the book figured out that despite the death he has seen in Rwanda he can find permission to go on living. I thought, *That's it! That's my tattoo*. Permission to go on Living as Loved. It's Perfect.

Chapter Fourteen:
An Insider's Perspective

"Wait, ladies!" called a staff member. We were about ready to walk out of the door of the art studio. We had just finished art therapy for the day. The art therapist walked towards the exit and said, "We started with five pairs of scissors and now there are four. Does anyone mistakenly have them or has anyone seen them put away somewhere other than on the counter next to my desk?" I shook my head, *Nope*.

Some ladies asked, "Why would someone take a pair of scissors? That doesn't make sense."

I heard, "Are they in the pile of magazines for collages? Are they in the bracelet-making bin?"

I knew immediately what happened without anyone saying it: We had an influx of new residents recently. Someone didn't realize that we count scissors and had pocketed a pair. Probably to hurt herself. Takes one to know one. If I hadn't struggled with self-harm I'd have been asking the same questions as some of my peers about why the scissors were gone.

A room and pocket search ensued. The scissors were found in the bedroom drawer of a lady who was a new resident.

I walked into the bathroom. It was just after lunch and the MHC was standing at the doorway to help support and monitor for purging in the toilets. She was humming to herself and there was a lot of noise in the three-stall bathroom. Plus the water was running. *No one would notice if I puked really quickly,* I thought. I had finished my meal with Ensure, a liquid nutritional supplement, and it would be easy to puke up. I felt so full, like my stomach was a balloon about to burst.

My jeans were tighter; I didn't even need my belt to hold them up anymore. My legs touched when I stood naked with my feet together. The line from my ribs to my hips wasn't as crisp as it used to be; it had gotten softer. I didn't like the shape of my upper arms or that my stomach wasn't flat. Even my breasts felt huge.

At home I had arguments with myself about whether or not it was okay to have another tablespoon of hot chocolate powder in my cup. In my mind it was not just "another tablespoon," it was another twenty calories. On my hard days, my self-worth would hinge on those twenty calories. When I was really struggling, the five calories in a piece of gum counted. Even how far I walked from the parking lot to the store was factored in.

I used to buy foods that I didn't like so that if I couldn't restrain myself and I binged, I would hate it and stop more quickly. I made disgusting creations in the kitchen with combinations of fake sugar and whole-wheat flour. I went to the grocery store almost every day. I bought things that I didn't eat or didn't like so that when I ate I would feel okay throwing it up. It was a waste of money. It was always a win when I ate something and didn't like it and threw it away without finishing it. It was like my body was saying, "Yep, eating nothing is better than eating that!"

I knew that my body changed when I went from a starving-weight to a recovery-weight; it just felt really sad and really hard to go through the process. There was something alluring about starving until I literally disappeared. Something that felt safe about having one foot in the land of the living and one foot in the land of the dead. It was a back up plan. I felt safe when I was invisible. No one expected anything from me. I couldn't get hurt. I couldn't be criticized. I couldn't be seen.

Something inside of me grieved when I had to eat again. When I had to agree to be visible. Agree to choose life, one meal at a time. Something inside of me was terrified, horrified, and sad about agreeing to exist. Underneath all these feelings a little bubble of hope began to rise as dreams trickled into the space that recovery was beginning to inhabit.

I stood in the bathroom stall. *Would they notice my feet facing the toilet underneath the stall? Would they hear me gag?* I stuck my fingers down my throat and closed my eyes. I held my breath and tried to time the gag with a toilet flush. My knuckles rubbed against my molars and became raw. (Classic sign of a woman struggling with Bulimia: First few knuckles on the dominant hand were raw.) My nose was running. My eyes were red. I felt like shit. *Will someone call me out on this? What should I say? This is not who I want to be.*

Why did I just do this again? I thought. Shame and frustration welled up in my throat and I tried to take a deep breath while wiping my vomit-covered hands off with toilet paper. *I'm so stupid. Do I tell someone about this or not? Is that telling on my disease? If I don't tell is it lying? What do I do now? Fuck.*

God, I mumbled the beginning of a wordless prayer to God. I flushed the toilet hoping all traces of the purge would go down in one flush. Two flushes would look suspicious. I stepped out of the stall to wash my hands. I couldn't rinse my mouth because that'd be suspicious, too. I tried to appear normal and vowed to tell someone on my treatment team about this later in the day.

Chapter Fifteen: Reality Check

"My meds are going to make me gain weight!" I said to Ben, a therapist on my treatment team. "I just started Lithium and it is a salt. That means I am going to gain water weight!" I said.

Ben listened to me with the patience of a saint. "Lisa," he said, "you sound pretty worked up about this."

"Yeah, I am," I said. "And, I already gained all the weight I needed to. I am at my restored-weight instead of my starving-weight. I gained *thirty pounds* in ten weeks. I do not need to gain any more weight!"

"Can I challenge you with something?" Ben said.

I sighed. I loved people who challenged me. And at the same time sometimes it was challenging (naturally). "Yes," I said.

Ben started, "So, I know that you are passionate about helping people all over the world, right?" I nodded. I wanted to go into a career that allowed me to help eliminate extreme poverty abroad and work with the HIV/AIDS epidemic in those countries. Ben continued, "So, worrying about gaining weight because of medication is a very high-class problem, right? The fact that we *have* medication, that we *have* enough food to potentially gain weight, and the fact that we *have* clean water to drink to even worry about water weight."

"Yes." *Ugh*, I sighed. "I'm so grateful for people in my life who are honest with me. You are so right," I said. "You are so right. Okay, I will drink water even though I'm afraid it will make me gain weight." That was the perfect thing to say to me to put things back into perspective. Ben knew me well.

The first time I met Ben he was not on my treatment team. He was a discharge planner for some other residents at the treatment center. When I saw a male around the residence hall I immediately thought, *That is really creepy. Why would a guy work here with all women?*

Over time I got to know Ben and realized he was not creepy; he was actually pretty down to earth. And he was happily married and really just loved helping people. And he was good at it too.

The next time that I came to therapy with Ben I brought a photograph. It was a photograph from a news article on the BBC website. It showed the back, neck, and head of an African woman from South Sudan. She was holding a tiny baby over her shoulder. The baby was clinging desperately to the mother's neck and had a feeding tube coming from his nose. The little baby was so skinny that his ribs were clearly visible.

The picture moved me in several ways. One, I wanted to work to alleviate extreme poverty and the co-occurring problems that came with extreme poverty. And two, this picture was a picture of an innocent baby trying to live and survive. I told Ben how I realized I was blessed to have a problem where I could choose to not eat or choose to puke up my food. That was not a luxury for a lot of people. For these reasons I was instantly grateful when I looked at this picture. It helped me to put things in perspective.

"Lisa, life is a process. Getting to the life you want is a process," Moe said. Moe was a therapist whom I had become close to over the course of my trips to residential treatment. She was tall, nearly six feet. And she was a no-nonsense lady. Moe was very kind, and she was very direct with me and modeled excellent boundaries.

"I don't understand 'process,' Moe," I said. "I only know being not okay or being okay."

Moe was so smart and she said to me, "Lisa, you totally understand 'process.' Look at this art piece you brought to show me. How many layers are on it? How did you make this?"

I looked at the tree and elephant picture in front of me. "Well," I mumbled, "it was a recycled canvas, so there was a layer already on it. Then, I glued tissue paper squares on it. Then, I drew a tree with a permanent marker. Then, I glued a black elephant and some brown elephants under the tree. Next I cut out fifteen bigger adult elephants from the pages of a novel. I glued them atop the tissue paper. I put a sealant layer atop it. Then I put patterns with paints and the piece was finished."

Moe said, "See, Lisa. You totally understand process. That's how life is and recovery is: it's a process."

A week later I was trying a new fruit: a mango. I discovered that I loved mangos and I loved that they were a process to eat.

I walked over to Moe's office and said, "Moe! I get it. I finally get it. I do understand 'process' and I do like things that are a process." And I explained all about the mango. Recovery was a process; it was like eating a mango.

Moe and I had a very unusual experience meeting each other. I had asked for a pass to go to a really close friend's wedding. I was supposed to be in it. Moe was the staff member who had to approve the pass. Moe had said no. I was livid. At this point I had never met Moe and she was just this vague entity that existed somewhere on the treatment center campus.

The week after the wedding my schedule was changed and I was in a new process group. Moe and Ben were leading this group. I was so angry. I tried to maintain a demeanor of hostile and detached. However, when Ben asked me if I was upset and did I want to process it I exploded.

"Yeah, I am really upset with Moe. And she doesn't even know me and it's her fault I missed this wedding,"

I said.

"Wait, we've never met. Lisa, are you mad at me personally?" Moe asked. Assuming I would say no.

"YES. I am super fucking mad at you," my anger spewed out like a soda can shaken up and then opened. "It's your fault! You didn't okay the pass. And I think that's rude. And I don't like you. And I don't respect you. And I wish you weren't leading this group," I said.

"Okay," Moe said. "I'm glad you feel safe here to express your anger."

"Yeah, I'm really upset. I think this is stupid. And you ruined my chance to be in her wedding. It was really important to me. And you didn't even look into the situation. You just decided. You don't even know me."

As group ended and my anger plateaued I felt a little guilty at my angry outburst. And, I also felt that it was fully justified and legitimate. And I never planned on seeing Moe again, so I didn't really care what she thought of me. She deserved it in my book.

The next day I met with Marlea, the clinical coordinator of the treatment center. A week prior I had asked for a primary therapist change.

My primary therapist had been Teresa. She was an older woman. She was skinny, wiry, and wore a puffy down vest. Her hair was cut into a nice bob, but her skin showed wear and tear. I immediately guessed that she was (or had been) a smoker and had probably partied hard back in the day. I pegged her as a recovering alcoholic immediately.

She started off our first meeting by touching my arm and making a joke, as if we were old friends. Not okay. Don't touch me if you don't know me. And, don't touch me if you don't ask me first. A therapist should know that. That was the first thing that irked me.

Next, Teresa led me to her office and we sat in opposite chairs. She said, "Well, now lets talk about you." *Okay, that was fine*, I thought. *Give her some grace, Lisa. Give her some grace.*

"Why don't you tell me a little bit about why you are here," Teresa said.

"I've been in and out of treatment and I really want to work on my anxiety and my other issues," I said.

"Oh, I've had an eating disorder and I'm in recovery. I know all about it. I was in treatment over and over and over. I would just leave jobs. Just up and leave," Teresa said.

I was a little annoyed. *I thought she said, "Lets talk about you?" I think she meant, "I'm going to talk about myself." Did she think she was winning points with me by telling me she was an addict? That did not increase my fondness towards her. My dad was in recovery and it put a bad taste in my mouth for all things labeled "recovery."*

"Well, I can see how it would be hard to want to keep trying in recovery. You're tired of talking and tired of trying," Teresa said.

Why does she keep repeating herself? I thought. *That is so annoying. If she isn't sure about wanting recovery than why am I here? I do want recovery.*

"So, what do you do with your time?" she asked.

"Well, I am an artist and so I do creative things a lot," I said.

"Oh! I love making art!" Teresa said.

I felt like I was on a date and the guy was trying *super hard* to connect to everything that I said. It felt fake and ridiculous. And why did she continue to talk about herself!?

The last straw was about halfway through our session. Teresa pulled a stuffed bat out of her pocket and said, "This is Albert. It's almost Halloween and he wanted to join us for session. Is that okay with you?"

I slowly nodded and no longer questioned this lady's

sanity – she was decidedly crazy.

By the end of the session I had decided I needed to switch therapists immediately. And Marlea, the clinical coordinator, was helping me do it.

"I have someone in mind for you," Marlea said.

"Well, actually," I said. "I was thinking of Anka." My wish for her to be my mom could come true!

Sometimes I had fantasyland inside my head. I imagined that my therapists Moe and Ben would be my older siblings and I would get their non-work cell phone numbers. Moe and I could be roommates. I imagined that I would go to the dog park with Dr. Hailey and her new puppy. I imagined that Anka was going to adopt me as her daughter and she would be a mother figure to me. I imagined that I became friends outside of work with Mara and Melanie, MHCs, that I connected with. I imagined that the people on my treatment team were my new family and they loved me. I imagined that we would all go to church and lunch on Sundays after I got out of treatment.

As much as I imagined great relationships blossoming, I sometimes imagined awful things. If my dietitian was absent from work for a day or Anka was out for a week unexpectedly, then I would fear that they had cancer and were getting chemo treatments. Or that someone was mortally ill. I would imagine that someone got in a car accident or there was some other catastrophic tragedy occurring. My dietitian Andreea used to tease me, "Why can't you imagine I took the day off to go to Great America and I'm having a blast?" I would answer, "I thought about it. And, you took a day off during the middle of the week and it was raining and I didn't think you'd like something like roller coasters…" I obviously was using a lot of brain space on my fantasies. It was typical of kids who grew up in the type of environment I had to have rich fantasy lives. It was probably the reason my creativity with fine arts thrived.

"Well, I actually already picked someone that I think you will work very well with. And she has requested to work with you," Marlea said. I had no idea what she was talking about. "Could we ask Moe to come in here and finish this conversation?" Marlea asked.

"No." I said. "Why would she come in here?" I thought it had something to do with process group the day before and I wanted no part of that.

Marlea pushed, "Well, Moe has asked to be your new primary therapist. I think it would be a great fit!"

I almost suffocated. *What?!?! I just met this lady and yelled at her. And now she was my primary therapist?!! Oh no. This was bad. This was really bad.*

Marlea went to the door and asked Moe to come inside. I was so embarrassed I couldn't look up from the ground. I studied that carpet like I had a final exam on it the next day.

"Lisa," Moe said. "I'm really looking forward to working with you."

My eyes moved a few inches towards upward and my head gave a slight nod. I thought I was going to die of embarrassment. *What were the odds?! I thought. What am I going to do?!*

As the days and weeks passed I realize that what Moe and Marlea had done was genius. They realized that there was a huge therapeutic opportunity set before them. I was usually angry and guarded and did not let anyone get close to me. In this situation, though, I had opened myself up to be vulnerable. I had opened myself up to receive forgiveness and love and grace in a way that they hadn't seen before. I swore at myself about it. They rejoiced in the opportunity.

Moe stepped into the full potential of the moment and offered forgiveness. She took my vulnerability and held it with care. We became really close.

After awhile I thought perhaps this mirrored how God reacts to me. I can be as angry and spiteful as I want to Him, and he will take that vulnerability and hold it with care until I am ready to be in relationship with him. I thought it was beautiful. To this day I still call and email Moe and Ben every week. The relationships built in that vulnerability were deep and strong and would last beyond my time at the treatment center.

Chapter Sixteen: Shalom

One day I was reading through Luke and read the parable of the Lost Coin. It is part of a trilogy of stories each talking about things that are lost: the lost sheep, the lost coin, and the lost son. As I read the few lines telling the story of the lost coin my mind went to the art piece that I had lost last week in the art studio. Someone had taken it. I was really upset.

I had made this really cool tree and landscape with recycled objects. Obviously, it had been pretty good because someone decided to steal it. More than a year later this incident still had the power to irk me.

My lost art was just like the lost coin story that Jesus

told. Although I had all other canvases I had made and they were all precious to me in their own way, that stolen piece was still meaningful. It didn't mean that the rest were less important; it meant that my collection was not complete. That one piece was worth the same as the rest but the wholeness that having it would create was worth something, too. There was something about wholeness, or shalom as the Hebrew word expresses, that had an added value.

Maybe in lieu of an art canvas Jesus had a woodcarving stolen from his carpentry shop and that was how he understood the value of wholeness. Maybe Jesus became so wise on this topic by being so close to the Father.

Maybe the prodigal son story had a connection to this lost coin idea. It was a story of a father yearning for his family to be whole. The younger son who is lost isn't worth more than the older; his return merely creates the space for wholeness to exist. And when shalom exists it is a divine quality that reflects God. Maybe the way the father of the lost son feels is similar to how God feels about those of us who come back to him: he is so excited for things to be made whole again.

There was an article from the National Geographic Magazine in the September 2011 edition titled "Orphans No More." It was an article about the Nairobi National Park in Kenya and the work of David and Daphne Sheldrick.

They started taking in baby elephants that had been orphaned due to poaching. The elephants showed signs of posttraumatic stress. Over time, the elephants bonded with their human caretakers and began to heal. The humans needed to be careful to rotate caretakers so that each baby elephant bonded with multiple humans. In this way the elephants built a human family.

The baby elephants didn't do well if they only bonded with one person and that person became unavailable (for whatever reason) for an extended amount of time. The baby elephants experienced the absence of their caretaker as a big loss because they had already lost their momma elephant in the wild. One baby elephant even died from despair when Daphne left to attend her daughter's wedding and was away for three weeks.

When the elephants recovered (at their own pace) they were able to reintegrate into the wild. The baby elephants sometimes left and realized that they weren't ready to be in the wild and returned on their own to the nursery. Other times the elephant would come back with their newborn babies and show them off to their human family.

I loved this article so much. It made me think of my own journey: feeling abandoned by my biological family, going to treatment, building another family to heal in, and then leaving to reintegrate into the world. Sometimes I had left treatment and not been ready, too, just like the baby elephants that had left too soon and had to come back. Sometimes it took a long time and multiple times at a location focused on recovery to fully heal for both baby elephants and for those of us in recovery.

When I read this article I photocopied it and gave it to my whole treatment team and many of my peers. "If baby elephants can heal from trauma and build new families than so can we!" I told my peers. I started making elephant themed artwork and reading books about elephants. I learned that in a lot of ways elephants were similar to humans: they had strong interpersonal relationships, they mourned the dead, they had amazing memories, and they exhibited posttraumatic stress! And, most importantly, they healed from it!

Lisa Elefant

Eating Mangoes

Lisa Elefant

About the Author

Lisa Elefant – dreamer, artist, writer, activist, adventurer, child of God, and a recovering anorexic/bulimic addict. Lisa enjoys traveling, learning, backpacking, and creating.

Contact: lisaelefant.eatingmangoes@gmail.com

Lisa Elefant

Eating Mangoes

www.ingramcontent.com/pod-product-compliance
Lightning Source LLC
Chambersburg PA
CBHW031357040426
42444CB00005B/320